A Texas Perspective

I don't live on a ranch, but have friends who do. I wear loafers and sneakers as often as I do boots. I have only seen one tumbleweed but not one jackalope. I thrive on high skies and wild flowers. I respect the land. I believe that pride in one's state is a gift given from our predecessors, and it needs to be preserved and passed on. I celebrate our flag, our heritage, cultures and customs. I believe living here is a priviledge with responsibilities. I respect my neighbor. Everyone here is either family, friend or a friend to be made. I belive diversity is a blessing, courtesy a requirement, and character development an art form. I listen to classical, jazz, oldies as well as country music. I am not better, stronger nor more intelligent for living here, just fortunate. My smile is real, and when I say, "have a good day," I really mean it. I love my country, and I love my state.

My name is Paul, and I am a Texan.

iii

The Best of Texas Cooking

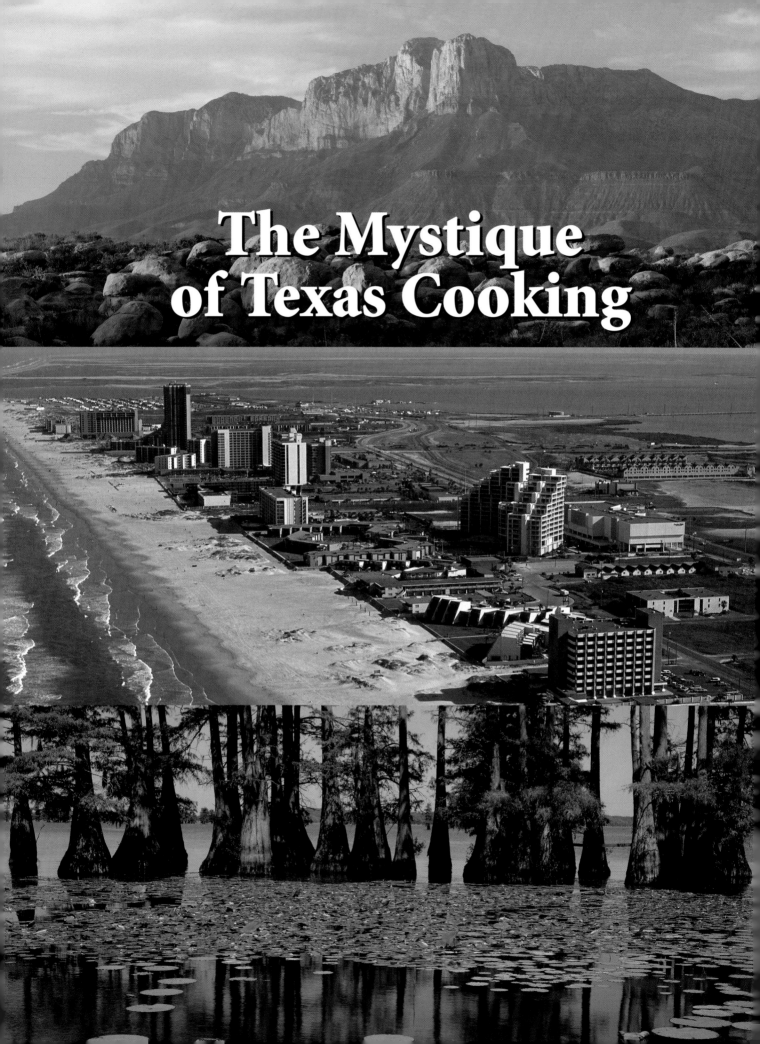

The Mystique of Texas Cooking

The land that became Texas was homesteaded by many cultures from many distant and different corners of the world, and, through the decades, the foods, the flavors, the hand-me-down recipes they brought with them have been carefully blended into the culinary heritage of a state that's as comfortable with sauerbraten and gumbo as it is with enchiladas, hoppin' john and ribeye steaks.

When the French stepped ashore, carrying the first flag to fly over Texas, they discovered that the abundance of shellfish along the Gulf coast could easily become the base for oyster stew and shrimp gumbo. After a while, they began adding sassafras powder to thicken their coastal concoction, creating gumbo filet. Native Americans had long been drying the herbal sassafras leaves and pounding them into powder on a stone mortar. The French felt right at home on the coastline. After all, those marshlands were ideal for growing rice, which soon became a staple of their cuisine in a New World.

The French influence can also be tasted in jambalaya, an aromatic assortment of delicate seasonings and herbs that include shrimp and oysters, perhaps chicken, and sometimes even bacon or ham. And those early French settlers were forever serious about their coffee. It needed to be black. It needed to be strong. It was never considered to be a luxury, only a necessity. When blessed with a slug of brandy, the coffee was said to keep away chills or fever, maybe even adding a few years to their lives. To Texas, the French left a legacy of gumbo, dirty rice and beignets. They later got together with the Spanish, and the magical blend of their cooking became known and respected as Creole.

Spanish missionaries trudged into East Texas to spread the gospel of Christianity to Native Americans, who, in turn, showed them how to raise corn, beans and melons, sometimes feeding them, according to old diaries, tamales and mush. The early colonists from Spain depended on the woodlands around them for survival, combining their old world recipes with turkey, buffalo, deer, antelope, plums, persimmons, berries and wild grapes. But always they regarded corn as the foundation for most of their meals, even though a British diplomat, who joined a Spanish family for dinner, reported, "Eating cornbread is like eating cooked sawdust." In time, corn was gradually replaced in their diet by rice.

The Spanish developed a process for squeezing certain stalks of corn and making a sweet syrup. And many of the pioneers cherished the lowly persimmon. Women favored a persimmon pudding,

and the men would fight over a good, warm persimmon beer.

Mexico turned Texas cooking hot, being responsible for adding chilies, coriander, comino seeds, oregano and garlic to just about every corn and bean dish that reached a Texas table. Mexico's political control of the region only lasted from 1821 to 1836, but its brand still heats up Texas foods. In fact, tortillas, chalupas, frijoles and chili con carne are synonymous with Texas cooking. Many of those who settled the Texas frontier firmly believed that chili, when it was hot and strong, and it was always hot and strong, could protect them against colds and malaria, as well as clarify their blood. Others simply swore that a good bowl of chili was an effective aphrodesiac.

After Texas became a Republic, it made a strong, bold and concerted effort to attract immigrants from Europe. After all, Texas had land, lots of land. And those Scandinavians, Czechoslovakians, Germans, Italians and Polish who journeyed to Texas shores brought seeds for the farmlands and new ideas for the kitchen.

The Czechs prepared kolaches. The Italian pioneer women taught their daughters the fine art of preparing pasta. For the Germans, wurst was always best. The Polish pickled their pepper beans and made herb pies. And the Asians made a delicacy out of bean sprouts.

During those years when the storm clouds of Civil War hovered above the landscape, Texas adapted to old-fashioned, Deep-South and Western cooking. African-Americans, working in the fields, introduced hoppin' john and hoe cakes. When lunch came, they simply baked their bread on the blade of a hoe held over a campfire.

Texans with a down-home Southern background preferred hog jowls and turnip greens, grits, crackling cornbread, okra either boiled or fried and hush puppies—cornmeal muffins that were created, so the rumor persists, to throw to the dogs around a campfire at night in order to keep them quiet.

Texas cooking is a proud reflection of its past. The recipes may change with the passing of years, but they will always have the distinctive flavor of the many ethnic groups who carved the state out of a rugged frontier and gave it the pride, the vibrance that mirrors the independent Texas spirit.

Those who would be Texans came from many nations.

Their culture was varied. So was their food.

Yet, in time, they became as one.

Prairies & Lakes

The Prairie and Lakes region of Texas is a curious blending of antiquity and aristocracy, a land that made its fortune on rich black gumbo farms lying in the shadow of great sculptured skylines.

Fort Worth is true to its past, as Western as its storied stockyards, as vibrant as Sundance Square and Bass Performance Hall. Both are located in the heart of Cowtown's historic business district, restored to its original Victorian beauty and filled with restaurants, gift shops and galleries. Thistle Hill remains as the last of the mansions fashioned by cattle barons who made themselves and their city wealthy. On the walls of the Kimbell Art Museum hang the legendary works of such masters as Rembrandt, El Greco, Picasso, Matisse and Cezanne. The Museum of Modern Art reflects the odd mysteries, the contemporary paintings and sculpture of Picasso, Mark Rothko and Jackson Pollock. And the Museum of Science and History portrays the lore of Fort Worth from battlefields to barbed wire, from fossils to dinosaurs.

Dallas is electric with high fashion and high finance. Its Morton H. Meyerson Symphony Center anchors a 60-acre Arts District. Tucked away amidst the rocks, timber and architectural splendor of Turtle Creek is the Dallas Theatre Center, the handiwork of Frank Lloyd Wright, considered the birthplace of regional theater. Downtown, the infamous Sixth Floor has become a museum, looking down onto Dealey Plaza where Lee Harvey Oswald allegedly assassinated a President and forever changed history. Around the corner is the West End Historic District, filled with shops and restaurants. The heritage of Dallas is mirrored in the collection of houses, buildings, cabins and churches that cluster around the lawns of Old City Park. And the art deco buildings of Fair Park home of the State Fair, house the opera, ballet, symphony and theater that comes to Music Hall, as well as the Texas Hall of State, Dallas Garden Center, the Health and Science Museum and the Dallas Aquarium.

Between the two cities, the world turns upside down during the thrill rides at Arlington's Six Flags Over Texas, and the thunder of thoroughbreds echo down the tracks of Grand Prairie's Lone Star Park. Just north of Dallas, Addison and Plano offer a myriad of prestigious shopping opportunities and great restaurants. Dallas claims the Mavericks and Stars. Irving is home to the Cowboys. The Rangers chase the pennant in Arlington. And hard-riding, hard-luck rodeo cowboys find their way to the bucking chutes of Mesquite.

Cotton blessed the farmlands of North Texas, spreading riches to Waxahachie and Ennis, Greenville and Paris. The communities are linked to the past with gingerbread lace hanging on the eaves, the cupolas, of fine Victorian homes. Denton is proud of its Oak-Hickory Historic District. Canton's Trade Days assembles a down-home assortment of the aging and the elegant across thirty acres: farm equipment and depression glass, old quilts and older furniture, crafts and clothing, old-fashioned and new. McKinney's Heard Natural Science Museum features the natural history of the area, complete with fossils from the Cretaceous period and the artifacts of early man who walked the prairie 1,500 years ago.

All roads from Sherman, as well as Denison, lead to the shores of Lake Texoma. Grapevine, nestled in its own historic district, is wrapped by the coves and inlets of a beautiful lake, and its wine festival pays homage to the grapes, near and far, that gave the town its name. Granbury's lake has become a getaway resort, weaving itself around a 19th century town that remembers its past with the sound of music in its grand old vintage opera house. And Weatherford is perched on the edge of the Western frontier, its orchards thick with peaches and pecans.

The vast reaches of the Prairie and Lakes region are thick with traces of the past. Jacksboro has preserved the officer's quarters, guardhouse, hospital, magazine and barracks of Fort Richardson. Bonham's Fort Inglish Museum has become a living history exhibit of 19th century life. At La Grange, the ill-fated members of the Mier Expedition, those who drew the black bean and were shot, lie buried beneath a forty-eight foot tall monument. The War for Texas Independence began on the fields of Gonzales when the town's militia refused to surrender a little brass cannon, flying a flag that said defiantly: "Come And Take It." The cannon fired, and the dragoons from Mexico fled in confusion. One shot. One victory.

And Waco is home for the Texas Ranger Hall of Fame and Museum, a stirring tribute to a breed of lawmen whose deeds became the stuff of legend, the kind who quickly answered the orders of S.P. Elkins in 18970: "There's a fight going on. Everybody get there that can." Waco was the one place where the Old South met the New West, a time remembered by grand plantation homes rising above the river. Its museums spotlight Texas Sports and Dr Pepper, first concocted in 1885 in Morrison's Old Corner Drug Store, making it the oldest soda pop in America. And the Armstrong Browning Library contains one of the world's foremost collections of the poetry of Robert and Elizabeth Barrett Browning.

Possum Kingdom Lake

Dallas
Grand Diversity

Dallas is a culinary delight. Around 7,000 restaurants. More than 79 cuisines. Home of two of America's most romantic restaurants, according to Dining by Candlelight. Four- and five-star restaurants. Originator of the frozen margarita and the chicken fajita. The birthplace of new unique gourmet restaurants. The residence of choice for some of the nation's top chefs.

Regularly ranked the number one visitor and leisure destination in Texas, Dallas is also one of the most popular domestic business travel destinations in America and a leading convention destination. The city takes its hospitality seriously. In fact, one in ten Dallas area workers is employed by the industry. Visitors benefit enormously from the many choices available to them: 63,000 hotel rooms, 33 shopping malls, 40,000 annual live performances, 160 artistic attractions, six professional sports teams, a zoo, a world-class rodeo, botanical gardens, the legendary State Fair of Texas, historic entertainment districts and the largest urban arts district in the United States.

When planning a family trip, keep Dallas at the top of the list for Texas-size activity the entire family will enjoy.

Icreated this dish in early 1986, and it quickly became my signature appetizer on The Mansion on Turtle Creek menu. The name "Lobster Taco" perfectly illustrates the casual elegance that characterizes Southwest Cuisine. Its appeal is rooted in the combination of rich lobster and a simple flour tortilla. The salsa and salad garnishes produce an explosion of color that promises exciting dining.

Chef Dean Fearing
The Mansion on Turtle Creek

Lobster Taco

Chef Dean Fearing, The Mansion on Turtle Creek, Dallas • Serves 6

3 1-pound lobsters
6 (7-inch) fresh flour tortillas
1 tablespoon olive oil
   salt to taste
1 cup spinach leaves, cut into fine julienne
1 cup grated jalapeno Jack cheese
   Yellow Tomato salsa (recipe to follow)
   Jicama Salad (recipe to follow)

Preheat oven to 300 degrees F. Fill a large pot with lightly salted water, and bring to a boil over high heat. Add lobsters and cook for about 8 minutes, or until just done. Drain and let lobsters cool slightly. Wrap tortillas tightly in foil, and place in preheated over for about 8 minutes, or until heated through. Keep warm until ready to use. Remove meat from lobster tails, being careful not to tear it apart. Cut meat into thin medallions (or medium-sized dices, if meat is broken apart). Heat oil in a medium sauté pan over medium heat. Add lobster; season with salt, and sauté until just heated through, about 1 minute. Add spinach and wilt in pan, about 30 seconds. Remove pan from heat, and stir in cheese until melted and creamy, about 1 minute. Spoon equal portions of mixture into the center of each warm tortilla. Roll tortillas into a cylinder shape, and place each one on a warm serving plate. Surround the taco with Yellow Tomato Salsa, and garnish each side with a small mound of Jicama Salad.

5

Yellow Tomato Salsa

Makes 1 1/2 Cups

2   pints yellow cherry tomatoes or 1 pound
        yellow tomatoes
1/2   small onion, minced
2   cloves garlic, minced
1   jalapeno, minced
1   tablespoon minced fresh cilantro
     Lime juice to taste
     Salt to taste
1   tablespoon maple syrup (use only if tomatoes
        are not sweet enough)

In a food processor, using the steel blade, process tomatoes until well chopped. Do not puree. Combine tomatoes and their juices with onion, garlic, jalapeno, cilantro, lime juice and salt, mixing well. Add maple syrup, if needed, to balance flavor and sweeten slightly. Do not make ahead. Mixture must be fresh.

Jicama Salad

Serves 4

1/2   small jicama, peeled and
        cut into fine julienne strips
1/2   small red bell pepper, membranes removed,
        cut into fine julienne strips
1/2   small yellow bell pepper, membranes
        removed, cut into fine julienne strips
1/2   small zucchini (only part that has green skin
        attached), cut into fine julienne strips
1/2   small carrot, peeled and cut into fine
        julienne strips
4   tablespoons virgin olive oil
2   tablespoons lime juice
     Salt to taste
     Cayenne pepper to taste

Combine vegetables, oil, lime juice, salt and cayenne to taste, and toss to mix well.

Chef Stephan Pyles of Dallas, who wrote the best selling *The New Texas Cuisine*, is acknowledged as one of the founding fathers of Southwestern Cuisine and was the first Texaan inducted into Who's Who of Food and Wine in America. He has been credited by Bon Appetit with almost single-handedly changing the cooking scene in Texas. He has released his fourth book, *Southwestern Vegetarian*, and is consulting, writing, teaching and producing television cooking shows.

Rock Shrimp Taquitos With Mango Barbecue And Avocado Salsa

Chef Stephan Pyles, Dallas • Yields 16 Taquitos

TAQUITOS

1   tablespoon olive oil
1   pound rock shrimp, peeled and de-veined
1/2   medium onion, diced
1/2   cup red bell pepper, seeded and diced
1/2   cup yellow bell pepper, seeded and diced
1/2   cup poblano, seeded and diced
1/2   cup shredded Chihuahua cheese
3   tablespoons chopped fresh cilantro
2   tablespoons ancho puree
     Salt to taste
16   flour tortillas, cut into 4-inch circles and
        warmed

Heat the oil in a large sauté pan until lightly smoking. Add the shrimp, onion, bell peppers and poblano; sauté for 2 minutes. Remove from heat,

and stir in cheese, cilantro and ancho puree. Season with salt.

Place a heaping tablespoon of the shrimp mixture on half of each tortilla, then fold over like a quesadilla. Serve with Mango Barbecue Sauce, and garnish with Avocado-Tomatillo Salsa.

MANGO BARBECUE SAUCE

1   tablespoon olive oil
1   medium onion, diced
2   cloves garlic, chopped
1   habanero, stemmed, seeded and chopped
3   tablespoons cider vinegar
2   tablespoon light brown sugar
1   tablespoon pasilla puree
1   mango, peeled, pitted and pureed
1   cup chicken stock

Juice   of 2 limes
Juice   of 1 orange
    1   tablespoon dry mustard
    1   tablespoon Dijon mustard
         Salt to taste

Heat the oil in a small saucepan over medium heat until lightly smoking. Add the onion, and sauté for 1 minute. Add the garlic and habanero, and continue to cook about 2 to 3 minutes, or until the onion is translucent, stirring occasionally.

Add the vinegar, sugar and pasilla puree, and cook until thick, about 3 minutes. Add the mango puree and chicken stock. Reduce the heat to low, and simmer for 10 minutes. Whisk in the lime juice, orange juice and dry mustard and Dijon mustard; simmer for 3-5 more minutes. Strain through a fine sieve, salt to taste, and serve with the taquitos.

AVOCADO TOMATILLO SALSA
Makes about 1 $1/2$ cups.
    2   large avocados, peeled, pitted and diced
    1   teaspoon red bell pepper, diced
    1   teaspoon green bell pepper, diced
    1   tablespoon scallions, diced
    4   medium tomatillos, husked and diced
    1   clove garlic, minced
    2   tablespoons chopped fresh cilantro
    2   serrano chile peppers, seeded and diced
    2   teaspoons fresh lime juice
    3   tablespoons olive
         Salt to taste

Combine the avocados, bell peppers, scallions and half of the tomatillos in a large mixing bowl; set aside. Place the garlic, cilantro, serranos, lime juice and remaining tomatillos in a blender, and puree until smooth. Slow drizzle in the olive oil. Add the puree to the avocado mixture; combine thoroughly, and season with salt. Let stand for at least 30 minutes before serving. Serve chilled.

Arugula-Fried Okra Salad With Roast Corn Vinaigrette

Chef Stephan Pyles, Dallas • Serves 6
     2   large ears of corn, shucked
     1   small shallot, peeled and minced
     1   clove garlic, peeled and minced
     1   teaspoon white wine vinegar
   $1/2$ cup chicken stock
   $1/4$ cup olive oil
   $1/4$ cup corn oil, plus more for frying
          Salt to taste
     1   egg
     1   teaspoon milk
    12   okra spears, cut into $1/3$ rounds
   $1/2$ cup cornmeal
     1   pound arugula, large stems removed, rinsed
          and dried
     1   medium tomato, blanched, peeled, seeded
          and diced

Preheat the oven to 400 degrees F. Using a sharp knife, cut the corn kernels off the cobs. On a large, heavy baking sheet, spread the kernels in an even layer. Roast in the oven for about 20 minutes, stirring occasionally until the corn is lightly browned but still moist. Set aside to cool. Reduce the oven temperature to 300 degrees F.

In a blender or food processor, combine the cooled corn kernels with the shallot, garlic, vinegar and chicken stock; process until the corn is pureed.

With the machine running, slowly add the olive oil and $1/4$ cup corn oil. When thoroughly incorporated, strain the vinaigrette into a bowl, and season with salt. Thin with a little chicken stock or water if necessary. Cover and set aside.

In a medium cast iron skillet, heat $1/4$ cup of corn oil over medium high heat until lightly smoking. Meanwhile, in a bowl, beat the egg with the milk. Working in 2 batches, dip the okra in the egg wash, and then dredge them in the cornmeal to coat thoroughly. Fry in the hot oil, stirring occasionally, until golden brown and crisp, about 2 minutes. Using a slotted spoon, transfer the okra to a baking sheet lined with paper towels to drain. Keep the fried okra warm in the oven while you fry the rest.

Place the arugula on a large serving platter. Drizzle with the corn vinaigrette, and toss thoroughly. Garnish the salad with the fried okra and diced tomato, and serve at once.

Pumpkin-White Bean Chowder
With Roast Garlic Croutons And Pomegranate Crema

Chef Stephan Pyles, Dallas • Serves 6-8

CHOWDER

2 $\frac{1}{2}$	quarts chicken stock
1 $\frac{1}{2}$	cups white beans, soaked overnight and drained
1	medium (5 to 6 pounds) pumpkin
1	tablespoon corn oil
8	ounces bacon, diced
1	medium onion, diced
2	stalks celery, diced
1	carrot, diced
1	red bell pepper, seeded and diced
1	yellow bell pepper, seeded and diced
2	cloves garlic, finely minced
2	tablespoons chopped thyme
$\frac{1}{2}$	cup white wine
	Salt to taste
$\frac{3}{4}$	cup Pomegranate Crema (recipe follows)
1	cup Roast Garlic Croutons (recipe follows)
$\frac{1}{2}$	cup chopped chives

Preheat the oven to 325 degrees F. Bring $\frac{1}{2}$ quart (2 cups) of the chicken stock to a boil, and add the soaked beans. Lower the heat, and simmer for 30 to 45 minutes, or until tender. Set aside.

Meanwhile, quarter the pumpkin, and remove the seeds. Place 3 pieces, skin side down, on a cookie sheet, and bake in the oven for 45 minutes. Have a bowl of very cold water ready. Peel the reserved piece, and cut it into 1/4-inch dices. Bring a pan of water to a boil, and cook the diced pumpkin until tender, about 1 minute. Drain and plunge the boiled, diced pumpkin into the bowl of cold water. When cold, drain and set aside.

Heat the oil in a large saucepan over medium heat. Add the bacon, and cook for 1 minute. Add the onion, celery, carrot, bell peppers, garlic and thyme. Cook for 3 to 5 minutes, or until the vegetables become translucent. Add the white wine, and remove the pan from the heat.

Remove the skin and fiber from the roasted pumpkin. Cut into pieces, and add to the vegetables. Return the pan to the heat, add the remaining 2 quarts of chicken stock, and simmer for 45 minutes. Ladle the soup into a blender, and puree. Pass through a strainer, and return to a clean saucepan. Add the reserved diced pumpkin and the white beans. Heat through and season with salt.

To serve, ladle the soup into warm bowls, and garnish each with some of the croutons, the crema, the chives and a few of the pomegranate seeds.

GARLIC CROUTONS

Yields about 1 cup.

4	slices French or sourdough bread
3	tablespoons olive oil
	Salt to taste
1	tablespoon roasted garlic

Preheat the oven to 350 degrees F. Cut the crust off the bread, and slice the bread into $\frac{1}{2}$-inch strips. Cut the strips into $\frac{1}{2}$-inch cubes. Combine the olive oil, salt and place roasted garlic in a mixing bowl, and add the bread cubes. Mix thoroughly so the croutons are well seasoned. Place on a sheet pan, and bake in the oven until croutons are golden brown, about 5 to 7 minutes.

POMEGRANATE CRÈME FRAICHE

Yields about $\frac{3}{4}$ cup.

1	pomegranate
$\frac{1}{2}$	cup creme fraiche or sour cream
1	tablespoon heavy cream

Cut the pomegranate into quarters, and reserve on of the quarters for garnish. Squeeze the other three-quarters into a saucepan, and reduce to a syrupy glaze over medium heat. Let cook, then whisk in a mixing bowl together with the creme fraiche and heavy cream. Remove seeds from the reserved pomegranate quarter to use as garnish.

Addison

A Taste of Variety

Addison perfectly blends the diversity of a big city with the ambiance of a small town. It is a 4.3 square-mile town located on the northern edge of Dallas. The town of Addison is truly unique in the amenities and customer service it provides to Dallas area residents and visitors.

Addison offers abundant opportunities for dining, shopping and lodging. And it showcases more than 135 restaurants which feature a wide variety of cuisine and culinary themes, enough to satisfy any taste bud. Visitors will also find some of Dallas' most prestigious shopping in Addison, including The Galleria, Nordstroms, Saks Fifth Avenue and Valley View Center, all located within five square miles. Addison is also a great place for both business and leisure travelers to stay, featuring more than 20 hotels, ranging from the luxurious to the budget conscious.

Addison is also home to a variety of attractions, hosting special events throughout the year. Guests can enjoy a theater production at the Water Tower Theater or visit the Cavanaugh Flight Museum. Visitors certainly won't want to miss Taste Addison food and music festival, held each May, Kaboom Town, the spectacular annual Independence Day fireworks show, the North Texas Jazz Festival or the annual Oktoberfest celebration held each September.

Lee Fields, whose passion for Mediterranean cuisine flourished while studying at the Cordon Bleu in Paris, France, serves as executive chef of the Sambuca Jazz Cafe in Addison, which boasts exotic New American cuisine.

Chop Steak Roulade With Whole Grain Mustard Potato Hash

Serves 6-8

CHOP STEAK ROULADE

3	pounds lean ground beef
1	whole egg
1	cup bread crumbs
$1/4$	cup chopped garlic
$1/4$	pound thin sliced salami
$1/4$	pound thin sliced white cheddar cheese
	Salt and pepper

Continued on next page

In a mixing bowl, combine beef, egg, breadcrumbs and garlic. Season with salt and pepper, and mix by hand until completely combined. On a plastic-lined baking sheet, spread out meat mixture to a thickness of $1/4$-inch.

Lay out salami slices evenly over meat. Lay out cheese slices on top of salami. By picking up the edges of plastic, roll the ground meat over the cheese and salami to form a spiral pattern. Pinch each end to seal, and place on a lightly greased baking sheet. Let cool in refrigerator for 30 minutes.

COOKING THE ROULADE

Preheat oven to 350 degrees F. Place roulade in center of oven, and roast for 15 minutes. Rotate roulade 180 degrees, and roast for another 10 minutes. Remove from oven, and let stand for 10 minutes. Slice roulade and serve on bed of Whole Grain Mustard Potato Hash (recipe follows).

WHOLE GRAIN MUSTARD POTATO HASH

3	pounds red "B" new potatoes
$1/2$	cup unsalted butter
2	bunches green onion
$1/2$	cup whole grain mustard

Dice potatoes in $1/4$-inch pieces. In a saucepot, simmer potatoes in water until tender. Strain and let cool.

In a sauté pan, on medium high heat, melt $1/2$ of the butter. Add $1/2$ of the potatoes, and stir constantly until golden and cooked through. Repeat with other half of potatoes and butter.

In a mixing bowl, combine cooked potatoes, mustard and thinly sliced green onions. Mix completely. Hold warm.

Grilled Corn Soup With Southwestern Creams

Chef Stephan Pyles, Dallas • Serves 6-8

GRILLED CORN SOUP

4	ears fresh corn, partially husked
2	cups chicken stock
$1/2$	cup carrots, chopped
$1/4$	cup celery, chopped
$1/2$	cup onion, chopped
2	cloves garlic, roasted
1	serrano chile pepper, seeded and chopped
1	cup cream
	Salt to Taste
	Southwestern Creams (recipe follows)

Over low charcoal fire, grill corn for 5 minutes on each side. Remove from fire, and, when cool, remove husks.

In saucepan, place chicken stock, carrot, celery, onion, garlic and serrano chile. Bring to boil, and let simmer 5 minutes.

Remove kernels from corn with knife. Add kernels to stock, and let simmer 10 minutes longer.

Place all ingredients from saucepan into blender, and puree completely, about 2 minutes. Place mixture through strainer, and return to saucepan. Add cream and place pan over low heat. Simmer for 5 minutes. Keep warm while making creams.

CILANTRO CREAM

1	cup cilantro leaves, stems removed
5	large spinach leaves, stems removed
3	tablespoons milk (or Half and Half)
2	tablespoons sour cream (or creme fraiche)

Bring 2 cups water to boil. Add spinach and basil leaves, and cook for 30 seconds. Drain liquid and place leaves in ice water for 1 minute.

Place cilantro, milk and spinach in blender. Blend until smooth.

Pass mixture through fine strainer into mixing bowl. Whisk in sour cream or creme fraiche. Set aside.

ANCHO CHILE CREAM

1	small ancho chile
3	tablespoons milk (or Half and Half)
2	tablespoons sour cream (or creme fraiche)

Slice ancho chile in half, and remove seeds and stems. Place in 400 degree F-oven for 45 seconds. Remove from oven, and place in mixing bowl. Add warm water to cover. Let stand for 10 minutes.

When ancho chile has softened, remove from water, and place in blender with milk. Blend until smooth.

Pass mixture through fine strainer into mixing bowl. Whisk in sour cream or creme fraiche.

Here is a great Texas chili recipe born at Traders Village and prepared by Bob Coats with the Bottom of the Barrel Gang Chili Cooking Team from Irving, Texas. Bob is a CASI Terlingua International Chili Champion and two-time CASI Texas Men's State Chili Champion

Out O' Sight Chili

Serves 6-8

2 $\frac{1}{2}$ pounds cubed beef chuck tender, cut in $\frac{1}{2}$-inch cubes

1   tablespoon Crisco shortening

1   (14.5-ounce) can Swanson's beef broth

$\frac{1}{2}$ can Swanson's chicken broth

1   (8-ounce) can Hunt's tomato sauce

2   Serano peppers

Place the beef and shortening into a dutch oven, and brown; do
continued on next page

Traders Village
A Texas Treasure

Traders Village in Grand Prairie and Houston are Texas traditions, providing shopping on a grand scale while serving up some the finest festivals and special events in the Lone Star State. Traders Village flea markets are the largest in Texas with the best-rated RV Parks and is a delightful destination for family-style entertainment. The markets are home to thousands of dealers, RV travelers and more than four million guests each year -- all looking for a bargain or a special treasure.

Traders Village offers non-stop festival fun with such events as Native American Pow Wows, Auto Swap Meets and Car Shows, Cajun Fests, Live Musical Concerts and Bar-B-Que and Chili Cookoffs, to name only a few. Throughout the 37-year history of Traders Village, more than a 100 Chili Cookoffs have been hosted on-site, with more than 10,000 distinctly different chili dishes being cooked, judged and savored. This is what gives Traders Village the bragging rights to call itself the official "Texas Chili Expert."

11

not drain. Then, add the broth, tomato sauce and whole Serano peppers. Bring the mixture to a boil, then add the following:

FIRST SPICES

2	teaspoons granulated onion
$1/2$	teaspoon cayenne pepper
2	teaspoons Wyler's beef granules
$1/4$	teaspoon salt
2	teaspoons Wyler's chicken granules
1	tablespoon Pendrey's Fort Worth Light Chili Powder
2	tablespoons Gun Powder Foods Texas Red Chili Pepper

Cover and cook one hour. Squeeze peppers and discard pulp, then add:

SECOND SPICES

2	teaspoons Pendrey's ground cumin
2	teaspoons granulated garlic
$1/4$	teaspoon Gunpowder Foods Hot Stuff
2	tablespoons Gebhardt Chili Powder
1	tablespoon Pendry's Fort Worth Light Chili Powder
1	packet Sazon Goya

Adjust liquid level with remainder of chicken broth if necessary. Cover and cook 30 more minutes, then add:

THIRD SPICES

1	tablespoon Gebhardt Chili Powder
1	teaspoon Pendrey's Ground Cumin
$1/4$	teaspoon granulated onion
$1/4$	teaspoon granulated garlic
$1/8$	teaspoon cayenne pepper
$1/4$	teaspoon brown sugar

Reduce heat to slow boil. Cook ten minutes. Adjust salt, cayenne pepper and Gebhardt Chili Powder to taste.

Kent Rathbun
Executive Chef

Kent Rathbun's creativity, dedication and range of delectable dishes have earned a national reputation as an impressive and inventive chef. He has established a world-class restaurant in Dallas-Abacus, where he has developed a menu of New World cuisine, drawing on Southwestern, Mediterranean, and Cajun/Creole influences with an Asian flair.

Lobster Scallion Shooters

Kent Rathbun, Executive Chef, Abacus Restaurant, Dallas • Serves 3-4

2	ounces sesame oil
4	cloves garlic, minced
2	shallots, minced
1	stalk lemongrass, minced
2	ounces ginger, peeled and minced
2	pound lobster meat, chopped fine
4	tablespoons tamari soy sauce
2	tablespoons sambal chili sauce
1	bunch scallions, chopped
2	tablespoons mint, chopped
2	tablespoons basil, chopped
32	pieces dumpling wrappers
2	eggs, whipped
3	cups peanut oil

In a medium saute pan, saute in sesame oil the garlic, shallots, lemongrass and ginger until slightly browned. Remove from heat, and transfer to mixing bowl. Then, fold in the lobster meat, soy sauce, sambal, scallions, mint and basil.

Lay out dumpling wrappers evenly on a flat surface, then brush a thin layer of egg on each wrapper. Place a small amount of the mixture in the center of the wrapper. Then, fold the edges of the wrappers up around the mixture, and squeeze the edges to seal the dumplings.

Deep fry the dumplings in 350 degree F–peanut oil until golden brown.

Texas Blue Crab Salad

Kent Rathbun, Executive Chef, Abacus Restaurant, Dallas • Serves 4

2	ounces canola oil
6	cloves garlic, minced
2	shallots, minced
$1/2$	cup sour cream
2	ounces boursin cheese
1 $1/2$	teaspoons green tabasco
$1/4$	teaspoon Worcestershire sauce
1	tablespoon cilantro, chopped
2	tablespoons chives, chopped
Juice	of 2 limes
1	teaspoon salt
	Cayenne pepper to taste
1	pound crab clawmeat, picked

In a medium sauté pan, sauté garlic and shallots in canola oil until translucent. Remove from heat, and cool.

In a medium-size bowl, whip together sour cream and boursin cheese. When mixture becomes smooth, season with tabasco sauce, Worcestershire sauce, cilantro and chives. Finish with lime juice, salt and cayenne pepper to taste.

Mix in crabmeat, garlic and shallots, being careful not to break up the crab meat too fine. Place crab salad on a piece of lavosh, and serve as an hors d'oeuvre.

Mole Cake With Tamarind Anglaise And Orange Caramel

Chef Stephan Pyles, Dallas • Serves 6-8

MOLE CAKE

11	ounces bittersweet chocolate
10	tablespoons (1 $1/4$ sticks) unsalted butter
$1/2$	pasilla chile, seeded
$1/2$	ancho chile, seeded
10	tablespoons sugar
2	teaspoons canola or 1 teaspoon cinnamon
$1/4$	teaspoon cloves
2	tablespoons pumpkin seeds
9	large eggs
$1/2$	tablespoon pure vanilla extract

Melt the chocolate in a double boiler, and keep warm. Meanwhile, in a small saucepan over medium heat, heat the butter until golden brown, about 8 to 10 minutes. Set aside.

In the bowl of a food processor, place the chiles, sugar, canola, cloves and pumpkin seeds, and grind until super fine. In the bowl of an electric mixer fitted with a whisk, whisk together the eggs and vanilla extract on low speed. Add the chile mixture, and whisk for 10 minutes longer. Add the melted chocolate, whisk to incorporate and slowly add the butter until combined.

Pour the batter into 8 lightly oiled 4-ounce ramekins, and place in a water bath. Transfer to the oven, and bake for 13 to 14 minutes; the cakes will feel only slightly firm. Remove the ramekins, and keep refrigerated until 1 hour before serving. Cakes are better slightly warmed in the oven.

TAMARIND ANGLAISE

1	cup heavy cream
1	cup milk
3	tablespoons sugar
$1/2$	vanilla bean, scraped
$1/4$	cup tamarind paste
4	large egg yolks

Place the cream, sugar, vanilla bean and tamarind paste in a saucepan, and slowly bring to a boil, breaking up the paste with a wooden spoon.

Whisk the egg yolks in a mixing bowl, and slowly strain in the cream mixture while stirring vigorously. Return to the saucepan, and cook over low heat while stirring continuously until the mixture coats the back of a wooden spoon. Strain and let cool; keep covered.

ORANGE CARAMEL

$1/2$	cup sugar
1	cup water
1 $1/2$	cups freshly squeezed orange juice

Heat the sugar and water in a heavy saucepan over high heat. When the sugar turns from golden brown to amber, turn off the heat, and slowly whisk in the orange juice. The caramel may turn hard but will melt again when reheated. Turn the heat back on to medium, and cook for 20 minutes, stirring occasionally. Let cool completely.

To serve, spoon the anglaise and the caramel around the warm cakes.

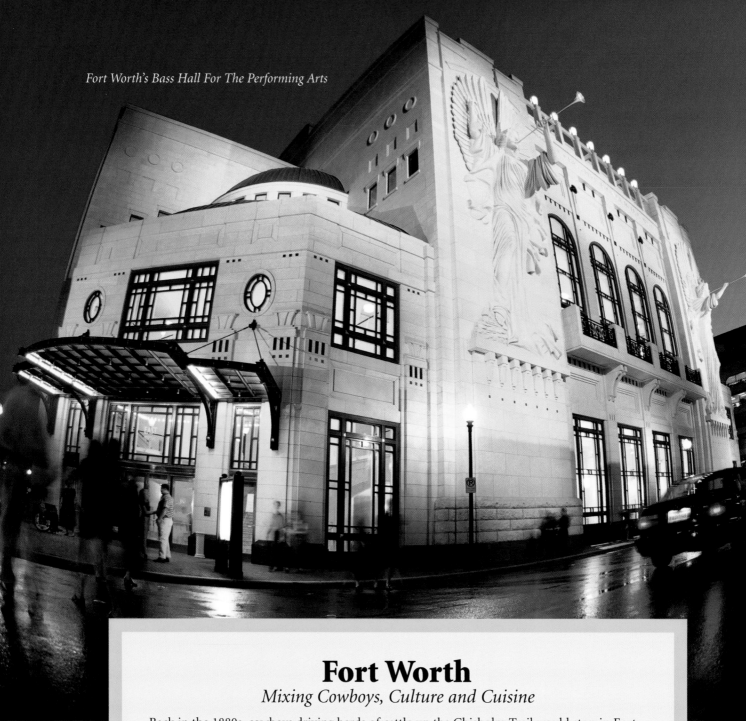

Fort Worth's Bass Hall For The Performing Arts

Fort Worth
Mixing Cowboys, Culture and Cuisine

Back in the 1880s, cowboys driving herds of cattle up the Chisholm Trail would stop in Fort Worth for a good time and a great meal. Today, visitors from all over the world stop in Fort Worth for its historic atmosphere, amazing cultural attractions, and wonderful restaurants and entertainment.

It's this mix of "cowboys, culture and cuisine" that makes Fort Worth unlike any other city in America. Here, you can relive the Old West. Explore an incredible variety of museums. See great performances in one of the nation's top performance halls. Shop and dine in the most exciting downtowns in Texas. Visit one of the best zoos in the country. Experience the thrills of NASCAR and Indy racing and a whole lot more.

From rodeo to Rembrandt, from water gardens to botanic gardens, from upscale shopping to down-home cooking, Fort Worth offers visitors a delicious menu of choices—every day of the year.

14

Grady Spears worked as a cowhand and cattle broker before becoming one of America's most celebrated chefs. He's the author of *A Cowboy in the Kitchen* and *The Great Steak Book*, and he founded the Chisholm Club, a landmark restaurant and cooking school opening in Fort Worth's Sundance Square.

Grady Spears

Frito Pie with Fancy Cheeses and Texas Pico

Grady Spears, Executive Chef, The Chisholm Club, Fort Worth • Serves 8-10

CHILI
4	tablespoons oil
2	pounds coarsely ground venison or chuck beef
1	cup red chili paste (see below)
1	red onion, chopped
1	tablespoon chopped garlic
1	tablespoon chili powder
1	tablespoon dried Mexican oregano
2	teaspoons ground cumin
2	tomatoes, roughly chopped
3	cups chicken stock
	Kosher salt to taste

TEXAS PICO
6	jalapenos, sliced and partially seeded
1	red onion, diced
2	bunches cilantro, chopped
6	green onions, chopped
2	tomatoes, diced
4	avocados, peeled and diced
	Juice of 3 limes
	Kosher salt to taste

CRÈME FRAICHE
2	cups whipping cream
4	tablespoons buttermilk

Combine the cream and buttermilk in a glass bowl. Cover and let stand at room temperature for 8 to 24 hours, or until thick. Stir well and refrigerate for up to 10 days. Makes about $2\frac{1}{2}$ cups.

RED CHILI PASTE
$\frac{1}{2}$	cup dried chili pequins
2	cups dried red New Mexico

chilies, seeds included, stems removed
$\frac{1}{4}$	cup white vinegar
$\frac{1}{4}$	cup minced garlic
1	tablespoon vegetable oil
1	teaspoon Kosher salt
$\frac{1}{2}$	cup water

Combine all ingredients in a food processor, and pulse until a paste forms. Store in a glass container in refrigerator for up to 3 months. Makes about $2\frac{1}{2}$ cups.

OTHER
1	large bag of Fritos
2	cups creme fraiche
2	cups grated cacciota cheese or jack cheese
1	cup goat cheese

PREPARATION
To prepare chili, heat the oil in a stew pot or dutch oven, adding onion and garlic until soft. Add the meat, and cook until starting to brown. Add chili paste, chili powder, oregano, cumin and tomatoes. Cook for 5 minutes, then lower the heat to simmer, and add stock. Cook on simmer for 45 minutes to 1 hour. Season with salt to taste. Remove from heat.

Prepare pico by combining jalapeno, diced onion, chopped cilantro, green onions, diced tomato and avocado. Add lime juice. Toss carefully, just enough to coat mixture with lime juice. Add salt to taste.

Into serving bowls, pile Fritos, chili, pico and grated cheese, and top with creme fraiche. Or set out all ingredients, and let guests build their own bowls.

Dry-Aged Rib Eye with Bandera Butter

Grady Spears, Executive Chef, The Chisholm Club, Fort Worth • Serves 4

- 4 (16-ounce) dry-aged rib eye steaks
- 4 tablespoons vegetable oil, divided
- $1\frac{1}{2}$ cups light brown sugar
- $\frac{1}{4}$ cup Kosher salt
- $\frac{1}{4}$ cup coarsely ground black pepper

Bandera Butter:

- 2 cups butter, softened
- $\frac{1}{2}$ cup chopped cilantro leaves
- 2 tablespoons Kosher salt
- 3 garlic leaves, minced
- 5 oven-dried or sundried tomatoes, rehydrated and chopped

To prepare butter, combine butter, chopped cilantro, dried tomato and salt in a large bowl or mixing bowl, food processor or a mixer fitted with a paddle attachment. Combine well. Remove butter bowl, and spread into a log $1\frac{1}{2}$-inches wide. Roll into cylinder, removing any air pockets as you fold parchment or wax paper around, tying off ends with rubber bands or freezer tape. Place in freezer one hour before serving; slice pats of butter off as needed to put on top of steaks.

In a large bowl, combine brown sugar, salt and pepper. Put 2 tablespoons oil in another bowl. Using your hands, coat each of the steaks in the bowl with the vegetable oil. One at a time, place steaks in the bowl with the sugar mixture, and coat the steaks well. Heat oven to 500 degrees F. Heat remaining 2 tablespoons of oil in a large skillet over high heat until smoking. Put steaks in the skillet, and sear for about 3 minutes on each side. Transfer steaks to a baking sheet, and finish in oven, cooking about 8 minutes for medium rare.

Remove from oven, and let rest for 5 minutes before serving. Top with slices of Bandera Butter.

Tenderloin of Beef Stuffed With Portobello Mushrooms

Richard Chamberlain, Chef, Chamberlain's Prime Chop House, Addison • Serves 4

- 2 (12-ounce) center cut tenderloins
- 1 portobello mushroom, diced
- $\frac{1}{4}$ cup chopped shallots
- 2 tablespoons butter
  Salt to taste
- 2 tablespoons olive oil

Preheat oven to 375 degrees F. In sauté pan over medium heat, add oil and butter, then shallots. Sauté for one minute (do not burn). Add mushrooms and continue cooking until all water for mushrooms is evaporated. Using a long, thin knife, make a $1\frac{1}{2}$-inch incision down the center of the tenderloin (lengthwise). Using your index finger, or two forks, stuff mushroom mixture in tenderloin. Season exterior of tenderloin, and sear in sauté pan over medium high heat in 2 tablespoons olive oil until brown on all sides. Place in oven for 8-10 minutes for medium rare. Cut tenderloin in half, and serve.

Mexican Shrimp Cocktail

Dennis Dial, Owner, Cafe Gecko, Addison • Makes 4 cups

- 1 pound cooked, peeled shrimp (any size)

ADD TO

- $\frac{1}{4}$ diced red onion
- 1 diced jalapeno (no seeds)
- 2 diced tomatoes
- $\frac{1}{4}$ cup chopped cilantro
- $\frac{1}{8}$ cup white vinegar
- $\frac{1}{4}$ cup salad oil
- $\frac{1}{2}$ teaspoon salt
- 1 pinch white pepper (or more)
- $\frac{1}{8}$ cup lime juice (or a little less)
- $\frac{1}{4}$ (12-ounce) bottle catsup
- $\frac{1}{4}$ cup orange juice

Mix all ingredients, and chill with shrimp. Serve with tortilla chips or saltines.

Tim Love is chef and owner of The Lonesome Dove, a Western bistro in the Fort Worth Stockyards that combines the feel of the Old West with elegant dining. The restaurant has received national acclaim, including praise by the *New York Times* for its stylish Western theme.

Roasted Garlic Stuffed Beef Tenderloin With Western Plaid Hash and Syrah Demi-Glace

Tim Love, Owner & Chef, The Lonesome Dove, Fort Worth • Serves 4

1	cup Australian syrah wine
4	each beef tenderloin filets
10	each whole cloves roasted garlic
$\frac{1}{2}$	gallon peanut oil
2	each russet potatoes
1	cup julienne red pepper
1	cup julienne red onion
1	cup julienne green cabbage
1	cup julienne red cabbage
2	cups veal stock, reduced by $\frac{1}{2}$
$\frac{1}{4}$	cup minced jalapeno
	Kosher salt and cracked fresh pepper
1	cup olive oil

In a sauce pot, add $\frac{1}{2}$ cup wine, and bring to a boil. After $\frac{1}{2}$ has evaporated, add veal stock, and simmer until ready to use. Make a small slit in the

Roasted Garlic Stuffed Beef Tenderloin With Western Plaid Hash and Syrah Demi-Glace

Tim Love

side of each tenderloin with a paring knife, and stuff 1 large clove of garlic in each, and set aside. In a 4 quart sauce pan, add peanut oil, and heat to 325 degrees F.

On a mandolin or by hand, julienne the potatoes to $\frac{1}{4}$-inch strips, and place in cool water to remove some of the starch. When oil reaches 325 degrees, carefully drop potatoes in oil, stirring frequently. Cook for approximately 4 minutes, or until golden brown. Remove from oil, place in a bowl and season with salt and pepper.

In a large, hot iron skillet or flat grill, put $\frac{1}{2}$ cup olive oil, and add both peppers, cabbage, onions and remainder of garlic. Cook until cabbage is wilted, adding salt and pepper to taste. Add remainder of wine to cabbage mixture, and simmer.

In a hot sauté pan, add $\frac{1}{4}$ cup olive oil. Season filets by rubbing the salt and pepper into the top and bottom of the steak. Place all four steaks in the pan at once, and sear on high for $1\frac{1}{2}$ minutes each side, and place in a 350 degree F-oven for 4 minutes for medium rare to medium.

To plate, place potatoes in center of plate, and add the cabbage on top. Place tenderloin on top of the cabbage, and pour veal stock on top of the steak. Garnish with a seasonal green vegetable like asparagus or green beans.

Champagne Risotto

Tim Love, Owner & Chef, The Lonesome Dove,
Fort Worth • Serves 4

$1/2$ cup olive oil
1 $1/2$ pounds butter
3 cups onions
3 pounds Arborio rice
2 quarts chicken stock
Salt and pepper to taste
2 bottles champagne
$1/2$ cup Parmesan cheese

Heat olive oil and butter in a large pot. Add onions and saute until transparent. Add rice and saute until golden. Add chicken stock two cups at a time, stirring constantly with a WOODEN SPOON until all is absorbed. Using the same method, add champagne, two cups at a time. Salt and pepper to taste. Add cheese and heat until absorbed by the rice.

Cannelloni Stuffed With Chicken And Roasted Potatoes

Jane and Franchesco Secchi, Owners, Ferrari's Villa,
Addison • Serves 3-4

1 pound breast of chicken, diced
$1/2$ pound fresh spinach
1 stalk celery, chopped
1 medium carrot, chopped
2 tablespoons garlic, chopped
1 teaspoon black pepper
Olive oil
1 cup dry white wine
2 tablespoons pecorino cheese
4 crepes
2 cups heavy cream
2 cups Parmesan cheese

Throw all vegetables and the chicken in pan with olive oil, and mix. Bake in oven for about 45 minutes at 350 degrees F. Remove from oven, and splash with dry white wine. Grind all cooked ingredients in blender. Add cheese. On each crepe, put about one tablespoon of mixture, and roll up. Lay filled crepes in baking dish, and pour over cream and tomato sauce, and sprinkle with Parmesan cheese. Bake in oven for about 15 minutes at 400 degrees F.

Smoked Trout, Avocado and Orange Salad

Serves 4

SALAD

2 smoked trout, about 7 ounces each
1 red onion, sliced paper thin
2 ripe but firm avocados
6 cups (6 ounces) loosely packed spinach or watercress leaves, or assorted greens, carefully washed
2 large navel oranges, peeled, white membrane removed and sectioned

To assemble the salad, skin and bone the trout. Separate the filets, then tear them into bite-size pieces. Set aside. In another small bowl, combine the onion and cup of vinaigrette. Set aside for 15 minutes. Cut the avocados in half. Remove the pits, and peel the halves. Cut the avocado halves into long slices $1/4$-inch thick. Place in a shallow bowl, and drizzle with cup of the vinaigrette.

In a large bowl, toss together the spinach or watercress and the onion slices (in their vinaigrette) with 1/2 cup of the remaining vinaigrette. Distribute the greens among 4 salad plates. Place the orange segments and trout in the same large bowl with the remaining vinaigrette, and toss well. Arrange the avocado slices, trout pieces and orange segments atop the greens, and serve.

GINGER VINAIGRETTE

$1/3$ cup peeled and sliced fresh ginger
$1/4$ cup (2 fluid ounces) fresh lemon juice
2 tablespoons white wine vinegar, or to taste
1 tablespoon sugar
$2/3$ cup (5 fluid ounces) peanut oil
Salt
Freshly ground pepper

To make the vinaigrette, place the ginger in a blender or food processor fitted with the metal blade, and chop finely. Add the lemon juice and vinegar, and process to form a fine puree. Transfer to a small bowl, and whisk in the sugar, peanut oil, salt and pepper (to taste).

A nostalgic ride around the courthouse

Granbury

Where Texas History Lives

Get away to Granbury, and relax in the peace of the past. You can stroll through the charming town's restored Victorian courthouse square—the first in Texas to be listed in the National Register of Historic Places. In fact, the readers of *Texas Highways Magazine* recently named it the "Best Town Square in Texas."

Granbury is nestled on a scenic lake in the Brazos River Valley, a place where you can fish, swim, ski and sail on sparkling Lake Granbury. Then pamper yourself in Granbury's cozy inns, waterfront resorts and quaint bed and breakfast hideaways.

Search for cherished treasures in the fine antique stores, gift shops and galleries throughout a historic district. Sense the simplicity of days gone by as you tour past grand old homes in a horse-drawn French carriage. And enjoy plays and musicals in Granbury's restored 1886 Opera House, or tap your toes to a live musical concert.

To top off your Granbury getaway, savor the flavors of the gourmet cuisine offered in Granbury's Texas cafes, tea rooms and eateries. You'll find everything from down-home cooking to Southwestern specialties and home-baked breads.

Pumpkin Bread

Merry Heart Tea Room, Granbury
Makes 8 Loaves

8	eggs
1 $\frac{1}{3}$	cups water
2	cups Crisco oil
2	teaspoons salt (level)
2	teaspoons baking powder (heaping)
4	teaspoons cinnamon (level)
4	teaspoons baking soda (level)
2	teaspoons nutmeg (level)
6 $\frac{2}{3}$	cups flour (level)
6	cups sugar (level)
1	large can, plus $\frac{1}{2}$ small can pumpkin

Preheat oven at 325 degrees F. Put ingredients in mixer in order. Mix continuously. Scrape down sides of bowl, and mix well. Divide into 8 well-sprayed pans.

Bake at 325 degrees F for 45 minutes to 1 hour, till top springs back.

19

Green Chicken

by Kathy S. Rice, Waco City Manager • Serves 6

3 $\frac{1}{2}$ to 4 pounds chicken, cut up
2 cups chicken stock
1 cup sesame seeds
1 large onion, chopped
1 clove garlic, chopped
Handful of fresh coriander
1 (10-ounce) can of Mexican green tomatoes (tomatillos)
1 small can chopped green chilies
2 jalapenos
2 tablespoons oil
Fresh ground pepper

Place the chicken in a covered casserole or pan; cover and poach for 45 minutes to an hour. Put in the refrigerator and cool until you can easily pull the meat off the bone. De-bone the chicken and put aside. Pulverize the sesame seeds in the blender or coffee grinder until as fine as possible, and set aside. Combine the onion, garlic, coriander, drained tomatillos (reserving the liquid) and chilies in the electric blender, and blend to a coarse puree. If necessary, blend in two lots.

Heat the oil in a skillet; add the puree and the sesame seeds, and cook for two to three minutes, stirring constantly. Add the liquid from the canned tomatillos and, if necessary, a little of the stock to bring the sauce to a medium-thick consistency. Taste for seasoning. Pour the sauce over the chicken, cover and cook over very low heat for 15 to 20 minutes. Serve with yellow or white rice.

Linguini Clams

Antonio Avona, Executive Chef,
Antonio's Ristorante, Addison • Serves 4

2 pounds baby clams
1/2 cup olive oil
6 medium-size cloves of garlic, peeled and chopped fine
1 teaspoon red crushed pepper
1 teaspoon oregano
1 medium red onion, diced fine
1 cup dry white wine
4 tablespoons sweet butter
15 springs Italian parsley leaves only, chopped fine
1 pound dried linguini (Italian)
Salt

Carefully scrub the clams under cold running water until very clean. Drain. Put in a heavy casserole cup of the olive oil over medium heat, and, when the oil is warm, add the onion, garlic, red crushed pepper, oregano; sauté for 2 minutes. Add clams and sauté for 2 minutes. Add wine and cover the casserole. Cook for 10 minutes, or until all clams are open. Add butter and the chopped parsley. Add salt to taste.

Bring a large pot of cold water to a boil, and add salt to taste. Add the pasta to the boiling water, stir with a wooden spoon and cover the pot until the water is back to a boil. As quickly as possible, uncover the pot, and cook the pasta until it is al dente. Drain the pasta, and transfer to a large, warm serving platter. Pour the sauce with the clams over the pasta, and toss very well. Serve with parsley on top.

Risotto Con Asparagi

Antonio Avona, Executive Chef,
Antonio's Ristorante, Addison • Serves 4-6

1 pound fresh asparagus
4 ounces prosciutto in one piece
4 tablespoons sweet butter (2 ounces)
2 tablespoons olive oil
2 cups raw Arborio Italian rice
4 cups homemade chicken broth
Salt and freshly ground black pepper

PLUS

2 tablespoons sweet butter (1 ounce)
$\frac{1}{3}$ cup freshly grated Parmigiano cheese

Clean asparagus and wash in cold water. Drain. Cut them into small pieces. Cut the prosciutto into tiny pieces. Put a heavy saucepan with the butter and oil over medium heat. When the butter is completely melted, add the prosciutto, and sauté over low heat for 4 minutes.

Add the rice, raise the heat to medium and sauté the rice for 4 minutes. Heat the broth until it comes to a boil. Then start adding the broth to the rice a little at a time, stirring gently, without adding additional broth until the broth already poured has been completely absorbed. After adding the second cup of broth, add the asparagus.

Season the risotto with salt and pepper. When all the broth has been added and the rice is cooked but still al dente, remove the saucepan from the heat, and add the butter and Parmagiano. Stir very well, and transfer the risotto to a large, warm serving platter, and serve hot.

Historic suspension bridge

Dr Pepper Museum Fudge

Makes about 36 pieces

1 1/3   cups of Dr Pepper
4   cups of sugar
4   ounces of grated
     unsweetened chocolate
4   tablespoons of white corn
     syrup
1/2   cup of butter (2 sticks)
3   teaspoons of vanilla
36   walnuts halves

Pour Dr Pepper, sugar, chocolate and corn syrup into a saucepan. Cool slowly, stirring constantly until sugar and chocolate are totally dissolved. Continue cooking on low medium heat until temperature is 236 degrees F, or until it is in the soft ball stage. Take off heat, and let cool at room temperature until it is lukewarm. Add butter and vanilla. Beat until it loses the shiny look. Pour mixture into buttered pan. Let cool. Cut into 36 squares. Place a walnut half on top of each piece.

Waco
The Heart of Texas

Waco is located in the heart of Texas where Mexicans meet Czechoslovakians, and everyone forgets that kolaches and enchiladas aren't authentically American. In the place once inhabited by the Waco Indians, many different cultures have truly been celebrated through good food. Waco's cuisine is the true treasure of the area, from egg drop soup to barbecue; the taste of Waco is worth the trip.

Beyond the great food, one can get lost in the natural beauty of the area. Cameron Park boasts 416-acres of tree-lined roads, limestone cliffs and nationally renowned mountain biking and hiking trails. However, if spending time with the gibbons and giraffes is your passion, a trip though the Cameron Park Zoo will make your day.

Texans are immortalized at the Texas Ranger Hall of Fame & Museum and at the Texas Sports Hall of Fame. Robert and Elizabeth Barrett Browning's works are brought to life through stained glass at the Armstrong Library, while The Dr Pepper Museum tells the story of the Waco-born soft drink. For a peek into the kitchens of yesteryear, there are five fully restored historic homes just waiting for you.

So, if you are the slightest bit curious, or hungry, point your car towards I-35. We'll be waiting with the table set.

Seared Sesame Crusted Tuna

Captain Glenn Cates, Executive Chef,
Truluck's Steak & Stone Crab, Addison • Serves 2-4

$1/2$ cup white sesame seeds
$1/2$ cup black sesame seeds
2 tuna steaks (8-ounce portions)
6 tablespoons clarified butter
Wasabi for garnish
Pickled ginger for garnish

Mix together both types of sesame seeds, and place in shallow bowl or dish. Place sauté pan on range or stovetop, over medium-high heat. Add 3 tablespoons clarified butter to sauté pan. When butter is piping hot, place tuna steaks into sesame seed mixture to evenly coat, and then into the hot saute pan with butter.

Cook each side 2-3 minutes until desired temperature is achieved.

NOTE: *We suggest cooking rare or medium-rare for optimum flavor profile. When tuna is cooked to desired temperature, remove from sauté pan, and transfer to a proper cutting surface. Slice tuna into thin slices, and shingle in the center of serving plate. Carefully pour Tamari Wine sauce (recipe to follow) evenly over slices of tuna. Add a couple of tablespoons each of prepared wasabi and pickled ginger around edge of the plate for garnish. These go great with tuna, but be careful. The wasabi is very spicy.*

Tamari Wine Sauce

Captain Glenn Cates, Executive Chef, Truluck's Steak
& Stone Crab, Addison • Makes $3/4$ cup

2 ounces rice wine
1 large shallot, finely diced
$1/2$ cup butter (unsalted), cut into small slices
$2\,1/2$ teaspoons Tamari soy sauce (Kikkoman)

Add rice wine and finely diced shallots to small sauce pan, and reduce over high heat until all wine is evaporated, approximately 3 minutes. Reduce heat to very low, and add butter slices one at a time until just melted.

NOTE: Make sure not to clarify butter while adding slices. Mix constantly with wire whisk or spatula to keep sauce from separating. When all of the butter has been added, remove from heat, and add the Tamari soy sauce. Hold in warm place until ready for use.

Chicken Velvet Soup

This recipe was made famous by the late Helen
Corbitt, who was director of food service at Neiman
Marcus. It was a very popular item on the menu of the
Zodiac Room and is reprinted form Helen Corbitt's
Cookbook, Houghton Mifflin Company, Boston
– Contributed by Stanley Marcus • Serves 8

$1/3$ cup butter
$3/4$ cup flour
6 cups chicken stock
1 cup warm milk
1 cup warm cream
$1\,1/2$ cups finely diced chicken
$1/2$ teaspoon salt, and pepper to your taste

Melt butter, add flour and cook over low heat until well blended. Add 2 cups hot chicken stock and the warm milk and cream. Cook slowly, stirring frequently, until thick. Add remaining 4 cups of the chicken stock and chicken, and heat to boiling. Season with salt and pepper.

Parker County Peaches & Cream Cheese Cake

Serves 4-6

Glaze
1 quart Parker County peaches
1 cup sugar
Crust
$1/4$ cup butter
1 cup graham cracker crumbs
1 tablespoon sugar
Cake
3 (8-ounce) Packages of Cream Cheese
2 eggs
$3/4$ cup sugar
$1/2$ tablespoon Vanilla

Peel and pit peaches. Cut into small chunks. Sauté peaches and 1 cup of sugar over medium heat until thickened. Set aside. After making the crust, strain the peaches from the glaze. Place glaze in a squeeze bottle, and refrigerate.

Melt butter and add to graham cracker crumbs and 1 tablespoon sugar. Mix with spoon. Transfer to large spring-form pan, and press evenly across bottom only. Place in freezer.

Blend on high, cream cheese, eggs, remaining sugar, and vanilla until smooth. Fold in peaches. Pour into spring-form pan. Bake at 325 degrees F for 45 minutes, or until center no longer jiggles. Remove from oven, and cool to 150 degrees F, then place in the freezer for at least 5 hours. Plate and garnish with glaze.

Parker County Courthouse

Weatherford
A Step Back In Time

Weatherford is just minutes west of Fort Worth, but it's like stepping back years in time. Weatherford has a rich western heritage. Did you know that two Weatherford Cattlemen were the inspiration for author Larry McMurtry's Lonesome Dove? Find out why Weatherford is called the Cutting Horse Capital of the World.

Stroll through Weatherford's historic district, with its majestic courthouse, built in 1884. Enjoy our historic square, and shop for antiques and rustic memorabilia. Visit the days gone by as you drive around town and see all the charming Victorian-era homes, or tour the "Castle on the Hill." The Texas Pythian Home was built by the Knight of Pythias for widows and orphans and is still used today for a modern day foster home.

Catch theatrical renditions of your Broadway favorites at Theatre Off the Square. Join family fun at one of our city or state parks, or maybe you would rather go golfing?

Be sure and come for Weatherford's First Monday Trade Days, always held the weekend before the first Monday in the month. The second Saturday in July is the Annual Parker County Peach Festival. Come enjoy some of the best peaches in Texas.

Visit one our lovely gardens, dine at a tearoom or café, shop 'til you drop or take our historic driving tour. Guided driving tours are available to groups of ten or more during the week.

Parker County Peach and Jalapeno Chutney

1st Place 2001
Parker County Peach Festival

1   quart Parker County Peaches
1   large Parker County Jalapeno, fresh
$^1/_2$ cup Parker County pecans
2   cups Sugar

Peel and pit peaches. Chop and place in large pot. Roast jalapeno over open flame until blackened. Peel and finely chop. Add jalapeno to peaches. Chop pecans and add to peaches along with the sugar. Bring to boil, stirring occasionally. Cook until thickened. Place into preheated mason jars, and pasteurize according to manufacturers instructions. Serve hot or cold on meats, cheeses, crackers, or just about anything.

23

Plano ... The Hot Air Balloon Capital of Texas.

Plano

An All American City

Welcome to Plano, Texas—an "All American City" located just 20 miles north of downtown Dallas and the largest city in Collin County with more than 250,000 people. No longer a sleepy little bedroom community, Plano has developed into a nationally recognized city, thanks to an award-winning public school system, extensive economic growth, numerous leisure and recreational opportunities and a quality of life second to none.

The Hot Air Balloon Capital of Texas features more than 3,600 hotel rooms, 700 restaurants, 70 shopping centers, an historic downtown, 86,000 square-foot convention center, exciting nightlife, Dallas next door, plus Southfork Ranch, professional sports and thrilling attractions like Six Flags just minutes away.

Chef Alain's Tiramissu

Makes one 9 x 9-inch pan

4	egg yolks
$1/2$	pound sugar
10	ounces mascarpone cheese
3	sheets gelatin
10	ounces heavy whipping cream
2	ounces Half & Half
40	lady fingers
5	ounces espresso
2	ounces Kahlua
1	ounce Grand Mariner

Whip heavy cream, and set aside. In a separate bowl, whip egg yolks with sugar until thick. Add the mascarpone. Dissolve the gelatin in 2 ounces of warm Half & Half. Cool slightly and add to the egg mixture. Fold in whipped cream. Add espresso, Kahlua and Grand Mariner to a small bowl. Soak lady fingers in the espresso mixture, and line the bottom of the 9 x 9-inch pan. Spread a layer of the cheese mixture over the lady fingers. Repeat a layer of lady fingers. Repeat a layer of cheese. Top with cocoa powder. Refrigerate for at least 4 hours prior to serving.

TIP:

This dessert freezes very well. We suggest cutting while frozen. You can then remove portions as you need and thaw to serve.

24

Grapevine
A City of Contrasts

Few cities in America can match the historic legacy, amazing diversity and unique atmosphere of Grapevine, Texas. The oldest settlement in Tarrant County, Grapevine is a city of history…a city of festivals…a city of contrasts. Home to the Dallas/Fort Worth International Airport, Grapevine Mills Mall, and Bass Pro Shops Outdoor World, Grapevine has one of the largest shopping and entertainment complexes in the Southwest…yet it is a place with a distinctly small-town atmosphere. Grapevine is home to the 160+ year old Tarantula Steam Excursion Train, the Grapevine Opry and six winery tasting rooms. Wine and grape growing keep Grapevine's agricultural past alive through an exciting, on-the-move industry. Texas is the 5th largest wine region in the U.S., and Grapevine is at its heart as the home of the Texas Wine & Grape Growers Association. Grapevine celebrates life, fine wine, exquisite art and delicious food. It is a place where your family can enjoy a variety of outdoor activities and indoor fun…and good cooking.

Please enjoy the following recipes from two of Grapevine's greatest cooks – Camille McBee of La Buena Vida Vineyards and Janeye McCallum of Homestead Winery!

Renaissance Glazed Chicken Breasts

Camille McBee, La Buena Vida Vineyards, Grapevine • Serves 4

4 plump chicken breasts, skinned and boned
Salt and pepper to taste
1 small ginger root, peeled and grated (about 1 teaspoon)
1 tablespoon orange zest (grate either fine or thick)
1 tablespoon olive oil

Mix Together:

$1/2$ cup chicken broth
$1/4$ cup honey
$1/2$ cup orange juice
$1/2$ cup La Buena Vida's Scarborough Mead

Spray baking dish with non-stick spray. Preheat oven to 350 degrees F. Place chicken breasts in dish. Salt and pepper. Add broth mixture. Sprinkle ginger and zest over all. Bake for 40 minutes or until chicken is plump and juicy. If it is not brown, place under broiler for 3 minutes. Serve with parsley rice and snow peas.

WINE NOTES: *This delightful honey wine is the perfect accompaniment for the sweet broth. After this course you will realize why the word "honeymoon" came from Mead, the oldest drink known to man.*

Ported Pears

Camille McBee, La Buena Vida Vineyards, Grapevine
Serves 3

3 Bartlett or Bosc pears, halved and cored
   Cinnamon mixed with brown sugar
   English Stilton Cheese
   Walnuts, chopped
   La Buena Vida's Walnut Creek Cellars
      Vintage 1985 Port

Preheat oven to 350 degrees F. Prepare baking dish with non-stick spray. Place pear halves in dish. Cover each pear with cinnamon sugar mixture. Fill center with English Stilton cheese and walnuts. Drizzle port over all. Bake in preheated oven about 20 minutes until pears are soft yet still a little firm.

WINE NOTES: *Enjoy with a glass of Walnut Creek Cellars Vintage 1985 Port. This wine is a perfect match with English Stilton cheese. The nutty flavor is a must with walnuts, and the age of this wine will relax you so you can linger a while over these sumptuous pears.*

Devilish Honey-Pecan Pie

Serves 6-8

$1^1/_2$ cups coarsely chopped pecans
1 (6-ounce) package chocolate chips
1 (9-inch) pie shell, unbaked
3 large eggs
1 cup honey
$^1/_2$ teaspoon vanilla
$^1/_4$ cup ($^1/_2$ stick) butter, melted and cooled

Sprinkle pecans and chips over bottom of pie shell. In a medium bowl, whisk together eggs, honey and vanilla. Blend in butter, and pour mixture into pie shell. Bake at 325 degrees F for 50-60 minutes, or until firm. Serve slightly warm, or at room temperature.

Pepper Steak Stir-Fry

Makes 4 servings

$^1/_2$ cup picante sauce
$^1/_2$ cup water
2 tablespoons soy sauce
1 tablespoon cornstarch
$^1/_2$ teaspoon ground ginger
3 tablespoons vegetable oil, divided
1 pound round steak, cut
      into $1^1/_2$ x $^1/_4$ x $^1/_4$-inch strips
1 cup fresh mushrooms, sliced
6 green onions, cut into $^1/_4$-inch pieces
1 garlic clove, minced
   Hot cooked rice

Combine first 5 ingredients in small bowl, set aside. In large skillet or wok over high heat, heat 2 tablespoons of oil until hot but not smoking. Add meat, and stir-fry 1-2 minutes; remove with slotted spoon, and set aside. Drain skillet, if necessary. Heat remaining tablespoon oil in skillet. Add peppers, mushrooms, onions, and garlic to skillet; stir-fry 3 minutes. Return meat to skillet. Stir picante sauce mixture, and pour into skillet. Cook and stir about 1 minute, or until sauce thickens. Serve over rice with additional picante sauce.

Hot Pasta Primavera Salad

Serves 6

$^1/_2$ cup no-salt broth
1-2 cloves garlic, minced
$^1/_2$ medium onion, chopped
$^1/_2$ cup frozen Italian cut green beans
$^1/_2$ cup frozen crinkle-cut carrots
$^1/_2$ cup frozen English peas
$^1/_2$ red bell pepper, cut into strips (or small jar of
      pimentos with juice)
$^1/_4$ cup fresh mushrooms, sliced
1 small zucchini, sliced in circles
1 cup fresh broccoli flowerettes
8 ounces tri-colored rotini, cooked as directed
$^1/_4$ cup celery, diced
12 ounces Italian dressing
   Tomato wedges to garnish

In large, non-stick fry pan, add broth, garlic, onion, green beans and carrots. Cook 3 minutes. Add peas, bell pepper or pimento, mushrooms, zucchini and broccoli. Cover and cook 3 minutes. Add the vegetable mix to the hot pasta, plus the celery and dressing. Decorate with tomato wedges.

Bastrop
Harvesting History

Bastrop's historical roots run deep. A rich harvest of classic Texas folklore and architecture exists today. Originally the site served as a meeting ground for the Tonkawa and other Southwestern Indians. It also provided a vital Colorado River crossing on the Old San Antonio Road – *El Camino Real*. It was not until 1821, however, that Moses Austin journeyed through the area and determined to build a settlement on the site. His son, Stephen F. Austin, fulfilled that dream after his father's death. He named the city and county in honor of the Baron de Batrop, who was instrumental in helping Austin create the "Little Colony."

Bastrop played an important role in Texas' battle for independence from Mexico. Eleven men from Bastrop died at the Battle of the Alamo. Bastrop came in second place as the choice for the new republic's capitol city. Numerous citizens of Bastrop achieved statewide prominence, particularly as leaders in early government and commerce.

Today, downtown Bastrop represents a unique blending of the old and new. Nestled on the banks of the Colorado River, the Historic District is filled with a variety of shops and restaurants. The historic ambiance of downtown is complemented by the nearby neighborhoods, containing more then 130 homes with historic markers and/or medallions. The Chamber produces a walking tour brochure with more detailed information on the Historic District. Visit beautiful Bastrop – you'll discover for yourself why we're known for the Lost Pines of Bastrop.

Bastrop's Colorado River

Spinach Madeleine

Makes eight $1/2$ - cup servings.

2	packages frozen chopped spinach
4	tablespoons butter
2	tablespoons flour
2	tablespoons onion, chopped
$1/2$	cup evaporated milk
$1/2$	cup liquid from spinach
$3/4$	teaspoon garlic salt
$1/2$	teaspoon cayenne pepper (optional)
$1/2$	teaspoon celery salt
$1/2$	teaspoon pepper
1	teaspoon Worcestershire
1	(6-ounce) roll jalapeno jack cheese, cubed
	Buttered bread crumbs (optional)

Cook spinach; drain and reserve liquid. Melt butter in saucepan over low heat. Stir in flour; add onion and cook until soft – not brown. Slowly add liquids, stirring constantly until thickened. Stir in seasonings and cheese, stirring until cheese is melted and sauce is smooth. Combine with spinach in 1 $1/2$ - quart casserole dish. (To double recipe, use 9x12-inch baking dish.) Bake 20 to 30 minutes at 350 degrees F.

Bryan–College Station
Rich In Tradition

Bryan–College Station, rich in tradition and history, truly is "smack" in the heart of Texas. The twin cities are nestled in the lush Brazos Valley, located 90 minutes north of Houston. The area boasts of big-city convenience with small-town warmth and hospitality, making it a business and tourist destination with a unique blend of cultural opportunities.

Bryan–College Station is home to Texas A&M University, the fourth largest university in the nation and a major center for education and research. A University rich in tradition, established in 1876, Texas A&M was first an all-male college until the 1960s when women were allowed to attend.

Bryan–College Station is also proud to be home to the George Bush Presidential Library and Museum. Built on 92 acres on the Texas A&M West Campus. The George Bush Presidential Library and Museum is not only an extraordinary research institution, it is an exciting cultural and historical museum. The Bush Library's collections include millions of official and personal papers, photographs, videotapes, plus 80,000 museum artifacts.

Messina Hof Winery and Resort is located in Bryan, Texas, just 15 minutes from the Texas A&M University campus. Although the Bonarrigo's, owners of the winery, are European, Messina Hof's soul is purely Texas. Tour and tasting are given daily, hosting more than 100,000 visitors annually.

Barbara Bush
Photo Courtesy of the George Bush Presidential Library and Museum

Barbara Bush's Barbecued Chicken

Barbara Bush, Former First Lady of the United States • Serves 4

Chicken:

1 (3-pound) fryer, quartered
1   large garlic clove, crushed
1   teaspoon salt
$\frac{1}{2}$ teaspoon freshly ground pepper
1   tablespoon oil
3   tablespoons lemon juice

Put ingredients in a heavy ziplock bag. Shake to coat well. Refrigerate for 24 hours if possible, turning the bag several times. When coals are ready, place chicken on the grill, skin side up, basting with the marinade. Cook until well browned before turning. (If baking in oven, bake at 400 degrees F, skin side down first.) About 20 minutes before chicken is done, begin using your favorite bottled barbecue sauce, or the following homemade sauce.

Barbecue Sauce:

$\frac{1}{4}$ cup cider vinegar
2 $\frac{1}{4}$ cups water
$\frac{3}{4}$ cup sugar
1   stick butter or margarine
$\frac{1}{3}$ cup yellow mustard
2   onions, coarsely chopped
$\frac{1}{2}$ teaspoon each salt and pepper

Bring to a boil, and cook on low heat for 20 minutes, or until onion is tender.

Then Add:

$\frac{1}{2}$ cup Worcestershire sauce
2 $\frac{1}{2}$ cups catsup
6-8   tablespoons lemon juice
    Cayenne pepper to taste

Simmer slowly for 45 minutes. Taste for seasoning. This sauce freezes well.

Yummy Green Beans

Barbara Bush, Former First Lady of the United States
Serves 4

1 pound of young, small green beans
4 quarts of boiling water
2 tablespoons salt or other seasonings
2 tablespoons butter or margarine
1 large clove garlic, crushed
   Salt and pepper to taste

String the beans, wash well and boil rapidly in salted water, uncovered, until barely tender and still firm (taste them to make sure). Drain and run under cold water to stop the cooking. Pat dry. Melt butter, add garlic and cook gently until softened. DO NOT BROWN! Pour over beans, and taste for seasoning. May be made ahead. To reheat, put in microwave for 2 minutes on high heat, or heat in saucepan over low heat.

Baked Beans

Barbara Bush, Former First Lady of the United States
Serves 6-8

2 (16-ounce) cans small baked beans
6 tablespoons catsup
1 tablespoon Worcestershire sauce
3 tablespoons dark brown sugar, packed
1 tablespoon dry mustard
3 tablespoons grated onion

Bake partially covered in a $2 \frac{1}{2}$-quart casserole at 325 degrees F for $1 \frac{1}{2}$ hours.

Cole Slaw

Serves 8-10

2 medium heads of cabbage, finely shredded
   (may add some purple cabbage for color)
2 medium white or purple onions, chopped
4 scallions, finely sliced
2 teaspoons salt
$\frac{1}{3}$ cup sugar
1 teaspoon dry mustard
$\frac{1}{2}$ cup cider vinegar
$\frac{3}{4}$ cup vegetable oil
   Freshly ground black pepper to taste
4 heaping tablespoons light nonfat mayonnaise
   or salad dressing

Sprinkle cabbage with salt, and let drain in a colander about 2 hours, squeezing as much water out as possible before continuing. May drain overnight if desired. Add onions. In a small bowl,

mix remaining ingredients, and stir into cabbage mixture. Adjust seasonings if needed by adding a bit of sugar first and, if necessary, more salt. Cover and refrigerate until ready to serve.

Red, White & Blue Cobbler

Barbara Bush, Former First Lady of the United States

1 can blueberry pie filling
1 can cherry pie filling

Place blueberry pie filling in bottom of 8 x 8-inch glass baking pan. Spread evenly and then place the cherry pie filling on top, smoothing edges of pan. Place in 400 degree F-oven to heat while preparing topping.

Topping:

1 cup flour
1 tablespoon sugar
$1 \frac{1}{2}$ teaspoons baking powder
$\frac{1}{2}$ teaspoon salt
3 tablespoons shortening
$\frac{1}{2}$ cup milk

Mix dry ingredients and shortening until mixture is like fine crumbs. Stir in milk, and drop by spoonfuls onto hot filling. Bake at 400 degrees F for 25 to 30 minutes, or until brown. Serve topped with vanilla ice cream.

Blueberry Pie Filling:

$\frac{1}{4}$ cup sugar
$\frac{1}{2}$ tablespoon cornstarch
$\frac{1}{2}$ teaspoon lemon juice
2 cups fresh or frozen unsweetened blueberries

Mix sugar and cornstarch in a saucepan, and add all other ingredients. Cook until thickened. Put into 8 x 8-inch pyrex bowl, and keep hot in 250 degree F-oven while making cherry filling.

Cherry Pie Filling:

1 can sour pie cherries
$\frac{1}{2}$ cup, plus 2 tablespoons sugar
$1 \frac{1}{2}$ tablespoons cornstarch
$\frac{1}{8}$ teaspoon cinnamon
$\frac{1}{8}$ teaspoon almond extract

In a saucepan, mix dry ingredients. Gradually stir in juice from canned cherries, and cook until thickened, adding cherries and flavorings at the end. Smooth cherry filling over blueberry mixture. Keep hot while making topping.

The Gulf Coast

The Gulf Coast

The Gulf Coast of Texas sprawls from the woodlands to the sea, its 624 miles of shoreline washed by white caps that spill inland from the Gulf of Mexico. Fishermen wade out into the surf. Shrimp boats are merely lonely silhouettes against the sun, their nets draped like a ragged spider's web around weather-worn hulls. And charter boats head toward an open sea to chase the elusive tarpon and marlin, seeking out those turquoise waters where snapper and mackerel hide away.

Houston remains a port city, connected to the sea by a fifty-one mile ship channel that has become one of the busiest waterways in the nation. It sometimes seems that the older Houston grows, the newer it becomes. Its magnificent Jones Hall raises the curtain on opera, dance, symphony and theater. The Alley Theater, an architectural showcase that some say resembles a castle, has caused many of the nation's top actors to leave the curtain calls of New York and Los Angeles and head for the Southwest. The drama of baseball is played out by the Astros, basketball by the Rockets. Broad boulevards, lined with grassy parks and fountains, leads from Houston's finance and energy empires to a green oasis that has become the city's cultural cradle with the Museum of Fine Arts, the Contemporary Arts Museum and the Rothko Chapel. Sam Houston Park is the final resting place for a cluster of quaint, historical homes and churches dating back to the 1850s. At San Jacinto battlefield, Texas won its independence. And at Clear Lake is NASA's Lyndon B. Johnson Space Center where Mission Control directed a nation's exploration of the stars. After all, the first word spoken on the moon when the Eagle landed at Tranquility Base was "Houston."

Galveston catches the seawinds that find their way past the waterfront to the Grand Strand, once known as the Wall Street of Southwest. It represents the country's largest assortment of restored iron-front Victorian commerical buildings, their streets lined with more than seventy shops, art galleries, boutiques, restaurants, museums and theaters. And its menus reflect the dockside heritage of Galveston: black lumpfish, icelandic caviar, smoked baby clams and escargots au natural. The tall ship Elissa lies in the harbor, and Galveston's East End Historical District mirrors the reflection of a "Gilded Age" of such revered architectural styles as Victorian, gingerbread, Italiana Villa, Romanesque and Greek Revival.

The good life reached Beaumont when the Lucas Gusher flooded the good earth with oil and ushered in the Age of Energy in 1901. The Texas Energy Museum offers a high-tech, eyewitness account of the region's petroleum industry. The Smithsonian Institute calls it the foremost energy museum in America dealing with oil and gas. Beaumont's Edison Plaza Museum contains the largest collection of

Palm trees shade the valley.

31

The Gulf Coast

Thomas Edison exhibits west of the Mississippi. The Babe Didrikson Zaharias Museum honors a Beaumont woman, a legendary Olympian and golfer, who has been described as "probably the world's greatest athlete, male or female."

Goliad's Presidio La Bahia, the oldest fortress in the Western United States, serves as a solemn reminder of the Texans who were captured and condemned to face a firing squad during their fight for independence. It now serves as a museum of the Texas Revolution.

Port Arthur claims to be the Cajun Capital of Texas, and its Cajun weekend is filled with hot boudin, gumbo, steaming crawfish and shrimp. Baytown owes its existence to the wildcatters who struck oil beneath Tubbs Bay. The scenic bays and sandy coves around Rockport and Fulton beckon fishermen with the promise of trout, redfish, drum, crab, shrimp and oysters. And Port Aransas became the quintessential fishing village of Texas after President Franklin D. Roosevelt came to the community in search of prized tarpon. The uncrowded beaches of Port Aransas are abundant with sand dollars and shells. Beyond them, tour boats head for the Aransas National Wildlife Refuge for glimpses of rare whooping cranes. If you've seen only a few, you've probably seen them all.

Corpus Christi is at forever linked to the gulf waters. Its Texas State Aquarium is home for more than 250 species of sea life—crabs, moray eels, octopi and sharks—captured in 350,000 gallons of sea water. At Heritage Park, the city on the bay shows off a rare collection of turn-of-the-century homes. At the futuristic Art Museum of South Texas, its windows, like paintings come to life, frame the sky, the sea, the boats that fade in the distance.

Corpus Christi is the northern tip of Padre Island, a scimitar of sand, curving down the Texas coast for 113 miles to Port Isabel. The tips of north and south Padre are crowned with resorts, but the long, isolated stretch in between is a National Seashore. Its pristine beaches capture the sun. Its surf has become a prime mecca for wind surfing and parasailing. And a new wave of civilization has changed the face of South Padre, one that clusters luxury hotels, condominiums and beach cottages together along the hideaway shoreline of the barrier isle. The southern tropical point of Texas has become a grand mecca for anglers, bird watchers and beachcombers. Shrimp and charter boats ease past the Port Isabel lighthouse, a proud beacon on the Texas coast, connecting the gulf to the palms, the gardens, the wildlife sanctuaries of Brownsville, Harlingen and the magic valley.

So much of the valley, particularly around Kingsville, is blanketed by the prairies of the famed King Ranch – so big that the seasons change on the north pasture a full month before they do on the south pastures.

The dunes of Padre Island.

32

The Gulf Coast

Fried Catfish With Collard Greens
Serves 4

Catfish

1	egg, slightly beaten
$1/4$	cup buttermilk
2	pounds catfish filets
$1/2$	cup cornmeal
	Salt
	Pepper
$1/4$	cup shortening or oil

Combine egg and buttermilk in a medium bowl. In another bowl, combine cornmeal and salt and pepper. Dip fish fillets in egg mixture, and then coat with cornmeal. Fry in hot shortening until golden brown, 5-7 minutes, turning once.

Collard Greens

5	bunches collard greens
	Salt pork
	Salt
	Pepper

Wash greens thoroughly, rinse each leaf at least twice and snap off ends. Fill large pot half way with water, add salt pork and bring to a boil. Reduce heat to simmer, add greens, cover and simmer for 30-45 minutes, adding water if necessary during cooking. Drain. Salt and pepper to taste.

Fried catfish with Collard Greens

34

Houston
The Good Life

Houstonians have a zest for life and an appreciation for diversity that's reflected in everything you see. And when it comes to great food, no place is better. Our international flavor is reflected in our outstanding restaurants. In Houston, you can find everything from French cuisine to down-home soul food. But delicious delicacies aren't the only reason to visit. Mild weather, endless shopping, a vibrant downtown and Theater District, a beautiful Museum District and some of the most exciting attractions in the county make Houston a truly dynamic place. It's not hard to see why we say, "Houston, you'll think the world of this city."

The Gulf Coast

King Ranch Chicken

Serves 10-12.

- 1 (2 $\frac{1}{2}$-3 pound) chicken
  - Salt to taste
  - Pepper to taste
- 1 bay leaf
- 1 cup chopped green pepper
- 1 cup chopped onion
- 1 stick margarine or butter
- 2 (10 $\frac{3}{4}$-ounce) cans cream of chicken soup
- 2 (10 $\frac{3}{4}$-ounce) cans cream of mushroom soup
- 1 (10-ounce) can tomatoes and green chilies
- 12 soft corn tortillas, torn in bite-size pieces
- 1 $\frac{1}{2}$ cups shredded cheddar cheese

Stew chicken with salt, pepper and bay leaf. After cooking, bone and cut chicken into bite-size pieces. In a large saucepan, cook green pepper and onion in butter until tender. Stir in soups on tomatoes and green chilies. In a 3 quart shallow baking dish, 13 x 9-inch, arrange alternate layers of tortillas, chicken, soup mixture and cheese, using $\frac{1}{3}$ of all ingredients. Repeat layers 2 more times. Bake at 325 degrees F for 40 minutes.

Peach Jambalaya

Serves 4.

- 1 green pepper, diced
- 1 onion, sliced
- 2 tomatoes, chopped
- 2 cloves garlic, minced
- 1 teaspoon thyme
- $\frac{1}{4}$ pound ham, diced
- $\frac{3}{4}$ pound smoked sausage, sliced
- 2 tablespoons oil
- 1 tablespoon tomato paste
- 1 cup chicken broth
- 8 fresh peaches, sliced
- $\frac{1}{4}$ pound shrimp, shelled, deveined
  - Salt and pepper, to taste
- 3 cups cooked Comet Long Grain Rice

Sauté green pepper, onion, tomatoes, garlic, thyme, ham and sausage in oil about 5 minutes. Add tomato paste and chicken broth; simmer 5 minutes. Add peaches and shrimp; cover and simmer 5 minutes until shrimp turns pink. Salt and pepper to taste. Serve over hot rice.

J-B Sausage Stir-Fry

Serves 4-6.

- 6 slices Texas Smokehouse Bacon
- 4 potatoes, thinly sliced
- 1 bunch broccoli, trimmed and sliced
- 3 carrots, sliced
- $\frac{1}{2}$ cup celery, sliced
- 1 medium onion, chopped
  - Salt and pepper to taste
- 1 pound J-B Smoked Sausage, cut into 6 portions

In non-stick skillet, fry bacon until crisp. Remove bacon and drain, reserving 1 tablespoon bacon drippings. Heat drippings in skillet over medium heat, add vegetables and salt and pepper. When vegetables are tender, place sausage on top. Heat covered for 15 minutes. Top with crumbled bacon before serving.

Shrimp and Seafood Lasagne

Serves 4-6

- 20 each lasagne noodles dry or
- 1 package fresh lasagne noodles, uncooked
  - Olive oil
- 1 pound fresh shrimp, peeled and deveined
- 1 pound fresh fish, scallops, crab meat, clams, combined
- 1 pound mozzarella cheese, grated
- 8 ounces Parmesan cheese
- 4 ounces Romano cheese
- 8 ounces fresh ricotta cheese
- 24 ounces marinara sauce

Cook the pasta according to package directions, drain, rinse and let dry. Oil your lasagne pan (pan to have at least 4-inch side) with a good olive oil. Then begin with the layers. First, one layer of pasta. Second, one layer of the sauce, then a layer of seafood pieces. The third layer more pasta, then, the fourth layer of ricotta cheese, a layer of mozzarella cheese and a sprinkle of Romano and Parmesan cheeses and lastly a layer of pasta. Repeat as many times as you have ingredients, making sure to finish top with layer of sauce and the remaining mozzarella. Cook at 350 degrees F for 45-60 minutes, or until top is golden brown.

36

Plant Sandwich

Rainforest Café at Katy Mills.
Serves 1

1   zucchini
2   roasted red peppers
$1/2$ ounce spinach leaves
1   portabella mushroom
    Focaccia bread (sliced in
       half widthwise)
1   cup romaine lettuce
    Caesar salad dressing

Slice the zucchini lengthwise into $1/4$-inch thick slices. Brush the zucchini and the portabella mushroom with your favorite olive or vegetable oil, and sprinkle with salt and pepper. Place on a heated grill or broiler and grill (or broil) the zucchini on each side for approximately one minute; grill (or broil) the portabella mushroom on each side for approximately 3 minutes. Bottled roasted red pepper can be found in your supermarket. Simply remove the pepper from
continued on next page

Katy Mills
A Shopper's Delight

Experience Texas' newest tourist destination! Katy Mills has introduced "Shoppertainment®" as the ultimate combination of shopping and entertainment for the entire family and is becoming one of the top tourist destinations in the area. Katy Mills is located very conveniently on I-10, only 30 minutes west of downtown Houston. Katy Mills is a one of a kind retail and entertainment destination, featuring 1.3 million square feet with 200 retailers, unique dining experiences and entertainment venues.

Retailers include OFF 5TH-Saks Fifth Avenue Outlet, Tommy Hilfiger, Perry Ellis, Liz Claiborne, Nautica, Timberland, Mikasa Factory Store, Geoffrey Beene and Lenox, as well as many others. Katy Mills stores provide tremendous variety and value oriented pricing. Interactive retailers include Bass Pro Shops Outdoor World, Jillians, Sun & Ski Sports and a 20-screen AMC Theatre. Restaurants include Rainforest Café, Johnny Rockets, Moes Bar & Grill, Lone Star Café, Red Lobster, TGI Friday's and Jillian's.

The convenient layout offers 26 giant video screens, themed neighborhoods, eight entrances and stunning architecture, all under one air-conditioned roof.

Katy Mills hours of operation are Monday through Saturday from 10 a.m. to 9:30 p.m. and Sunday from 11 a.m. to 7 p.m.

For more information call (281)644-5050 or visit Katy Mills at www.katymills.com. Shuttle service is available on Fridays, Saturdays and Sundays from major hotels in Houston to/from Katy Mills for $15 roundtrip. Contact Carrington Tours at (713)691-0885 for further information and schedule.

Mention that you found our recipe in the Texas Travel Cookbook at the Information Center Neighborhood 4 for a FREE COUPON BOOK worth hundreds of dollars in discounts.

the jar, and place on the grill for a minute or so to heat them up. Or, if you prefer, you can heat them up in the microwave. Place the spinach in a small bowl, combine the romaine lettuce with your favorite caesar salad dressing and toss lightly to coat. Toast both halves of the focaccia bread, and layer on half of the bread with zucchini, roasted red peppers, spinach leaves, portabella mushroom and caesar-coated romaine. Complete the sandwich by placing the other half of focaccia on top, and slicing the sandwich in half. Serve with your favorite chips.

Shrimp and Broccoli

Serves 2-4.

1	pound medium shrimp
	Seasoning
1	bunch broccoli
$^{1}/_{4}$	cup olive oil
4	cloves fresh garlic, sliced
1	red pepper, sliced

Peel and devein shrimp; pat dry and put into baggie. Sprinkle generously with seasoning, and shake, tumble or whatever it takes to cover shrimp with seasoning. Cut flowerettes off broccoli stem, and place into pot. Cover broccoli with water, and sprinkle with seasoning. Bring to a boil, lower heat and cook until tender, then pour into the colander, and run cold water over broccoli to stop cooking. Pour oil and garlic into skillet. Place skillet on burner, and cook garlic over low to medium heat. Cook until garlic is tender. Remove garlic and add red pepper; cook until pepper turns brown around the edges. Remove and save. Add shrimp to skillet. Cook until tender (shrimp turns pink). Reduce heat, add cooked pepper and broccoli, toss or stir in skillet until broccoli is warm.

Oriental Vegetables and Rice

Serves 4

2	teaspoons sesame oil
1	teaspoon vegetable oil
1	(16-ounce) package frozen broccoli, red sweet peppers, bamboo shoots and straw mushrooms
2	cups cooked rice
	Reduced-sodium soy sauce

Heat oils in large skillet over medium-high heat. Add vegetables; stir-fry several minutes. Add rice and 1 tablespoon soy sauce; cook and stir until rice is heated, gently separating grains. Serve with additional soy sauce, if desired.

Cajun Style Seafood Gumbo

Serves 4-6.

4	teaspoons roux
3	quarts water
1	large onion, chopped
1	bell pepper, chopped
2	cloves garlic, chopped
2	stalks celery, chopped
2	pounds shrimp, cleaned and deveined
1	pound crabmeat
1	pint fresh oysters
$^{1}/_{2}$	cup chopped green onion
$^{1}/_{4}$	cup parsley
2	cups rice

Dissolve roux in water over medium heat, then let boil $^{1}/_{2}$ hour. Add onion, bell pepper, garlic and celery, and cook over low heat for $^{1}/_{2}$ hour. Add all seafood, green onion and parsley, and simmer for 20 minutes. Serve over cooked rice.

Cajun Style Seafood Gumbo

Veal Chop With
Port Wine-Mushroom Sauce

Sean Moore, Executive Chef, The Steakhouse,
The San Luis Resort, Galveston
Serves 1, but recipe can be doubled to serve 2.

1	each veal loin chop, 14 ounces, bone frenched
$1/2$	ounce clarified butter
	Salt and pepper to taste
$1/4$	teaspoon garlic, minced
1	cup sliced fresh white mushrooms
2	ounces port wine
2	ounces heavy cream
2	ounces veal stock
1	tablespoon chopped parsley

Set a large skillet over medium high heat. Season the veal chop with salt and pepper, and brown both sides in the clarified butter, about 3 minutes per side. Remove chop from pan, and place in 375 degree F-oven to finish cooking (12 minutes for medium). Add the garlic to the pan, and cook briefly (be careful not to burn). Add the mushrooms, and cook 1 minute. Add the wine, and cook 1 minute. Add the cream and stock, and cook 1 minute more. Stir parsley into mushroom mixture, place veal chop on a warm serving plate, and pour mushroom mixture over veal. Serve immediately.

A Great Steakhouse
At The San Luis Resort, Spa and Conference Center

For four consecutive years, The Steakhouse at The San Luis Resort, Spa & Conference Center on Galveston Island has been named number four of Texas' Top Ten Steakhouses. The honor was awarded by Tom Horan's America's Top Ten Club, which receives recommendations from its members, as well as associate food critics and those in the food and beverage industry.

According to Horan, the steakhouses listed reflect the diversity, geography and entrepreneurship of Texas. The Steakhouse is the hotel's signature restaurant that features a unique blend of high-quality food, hospitality and atmosphere. The Steakhouse, with a menu showcasing Midwest grain-fed steaks, live Maine lobster, red snapper and lamb chops, features hand-crafted mahogany woodwork, leather furnishings and other luxurious amenities, including live entertainment.

39

The Gulf Coast

White Chocolate Eruption

Sean Moore, Executive Chef, The Steakhouse,
The San Luis Resort, Galveston
Serves 4

- 6   each whole eggs
- 5 $\frac{1}{2}$ ounces powdered sugar
- 6 $\frac{1}{2}$ ounces flour
- 8   ounces good quality white chocolate, melted

Butter and sugar the inside of 4 (4-ounce) oven proof molds. Sift into a mixing bowl the sugar and flour. Whisk in the eggs until just incorporated. Fold in the melted white chocolate. Fill each mold to $\frac{1}{4}$-inch below the rim. Refrigerate at least 2 hours, or wrap and store up to 3 days. Bake in a 375 degree F-oven for 12 minutes, invert to remove from mold and serve immediately.

Shrimp and Okra Gumbo

Serves 8.

- 2   cups fresh or frozen okra, diced
- 2   tablespoons oil
- 1   stick margarine
- 4   tablespoons flour
- $\frac{1}{2}$ bell pepper
- 1   onion
- 2   stalks celery
- 3   cloves garlic
- 3   quarts water
- 1   tablespoon Worcestershire sauce
- 1   tablespoon chopped green onion, optional
  Sprinkle of file powder, optional
- 2   pounds peeled shrimp
- 2-3   cups cooked rice

Fry okra in 2 tablespoons oil for 10 minutes, stirring constantly, as not to burn. Use aluminum dutch oven, do not use black iron pot. Remove okra and set aside. Add margarine and flour, and make a roux in same pot. Brown until chocolate brown, stirring constantly. Chop vegetables and add them to roux. Add okra and cook 5 minutes or until wilted. Add water and Worcestershire sauce, and then cook 1 $\frac{1}{2}$ hours. Add shrimp and cook 30 minutes or until tender. Serve with rice in a soup plate.

White Chocolate Eruption

The Port Aransas Marina

Port Aransas

Sun and Surf

Port Aransas ~ Texas' favorite "get away"! Located on beautiful Mustang Island on the central Gulf coast, Port Aransas has all the ingredients for a relaxing vacation. Find a cup of seashells while enjoying majestic sunrises on endless sandy beaches. Add a pinch of fishing from the surf, piers and jetties or on bay and offshore fishing boats. Spoon in some birding sites, and mix well with a tour of the town on the free trolley. Sprinkle on a little unique shopping at our coastal shops and boutiques, then top it off at one of many restaurants offering savory entrees and desserts. You'll have a recipe for fun and a vacation that will tempt everyone's palette. Visit Port Aransas, and do Texas ~ Island Style.

Port Aransas' Grilled Ling with Gulf Shrimp and Sea Scallops

Serves 4

1 $^1/_2$	pound ling filet, cut into 4 servings, or any other pelagic fish of choice
	olive oil
12	jumbo gulf shrimp
12	sea scallops, or substitute with fresh oysters
1	tablespoon olive oil
2	garlic cloves, minced
	salt
	fresh ground pepper
6	ounces fresh diced tomato, seeded (approximately 1 large tomato)
1	teaspoon fresh thyme
1	teaspoon fresh rosemary, minced
$^1/_2$	teaspoon dry oregano
$^1/_2$	cup dry white wine, preferably chardonnay

$^3/_4$	cup seafood stock (may substitute with $^1/_4$ cup low sodium chicken broth plus $^1/_2$ cup clam juice)
1	teaspoon fresh squeezed lemon juice
1	teaspoon Italian flat-leaf parsley, minced
1	tablespoon unsalted butter

Prepare grill. Pat fish dry, brush with olive oil, and season with salt and pepper. Grill fish for 5-6 minutes on each side, or until just cooked through. Meanwhile, in center of large frying pan, over medium high heat, add olive oil and garlic. Arrange shrimp and scallops in pan, and

continued on next page

41

season with salt, ground black pepper, thyme, rosemary, oregano, and diced tomato. Allow shrimp and scallops to cook approximately 3 minutes, turning often. Add white wine, and reduce by half. Add seafood stock and lemon juice, reduce flame to medium and allow sauce to come together, then add butter, and stir into sauce until melted. Finish with parsley. Arrange grilled fish on plates, top them with shrimp and spoon scallops and sauce over them equally.

Pecan Redfish

Scampi's Restaurant, South Padre Island
Serves 6

6 6-ounce pieces fresh Redfish fillets
    Coating mix – see recipe
    Egg wash – see recipe
    Sauce – see recipe
    Shoestring potatoes
    Steam fresh vegetables
    Deep fryer heated to 375 degrees F

SAUCE

1 14-ounce can low sodium chicken broth
$1/4$ cup clarified butter
1 cup pecan pieces
1 tablespoon flour
2 tablespoons Cajun spices
2 tablespoons Worcestershire sauce
$1/2$ cup honey

COATING

1 cup small pecan pieces
2 cups flour
1 tablespoon sea salt
1 teaspoon ground white pepper

EGG WASH

1 cup milk
2 whole eggs

Reduce chicken broth to 6 ounces, and cool. Meanwhile, in a sauce pan, add butter and pecans, and toast until golden brown. Add flour, mix and cook lightly. Mix chicken stock, Worcestershire, Cajun spices and honey together, add to pecan mix and cook for two minutes. Keep sauce warm.

Mix all ingredients for coating. Make egg wash. Prepare sauce ahead. Place fillets in egg wash then into pecan flour mix, and press fish with flour pecan mix for good coating. Deep fry at 375 degrees F for 8 minutes. Place fish on plate, and coat with sauce. Serve with shoestring potatoes and your favorite steamed vegetables.

Stuffed Mushroom Caps

Sean Moore, Executive Chef, The Steakhouse,
The San Luis Resort, Galveston
Serves 2-4

1 ounce minced onion, sauteed and cooled
6 ounces jumbo lump crab meat, picked
    through for shells
3 tablespoons fresh white bread crumbs
1 tablespoon heavy mayonnaise
$1/4$ teaspoon dry mustard
    Dash tabasco
$1/4$ teaspoon old bay seasoning
8 each large mushrooms, stems removed
2 ounces gruyere cheese, sliced

In a mixing bowl, add the first seven ingredients, and gently mix to combine. Generously fill the mushroom caps with the crab mixture. Cover each mushroom with a piece of gruyere cheese, and bake in a 400 degree F-oven for about 10 minutes (depends on the size of the mushrooms). Serve immediately.

Tracy Byrd Meatballs

Tracy Byrd

Tracy Byrd Meatballs

Serves 4-6

MEATBALLS

1   pound ground beef
1   tablespoon Worcestershire sauce
$1/2$ cup crushed cornflakes
1   teaspoon salt
1   teaspoon pepper
$1/4$ cup minced onion
$1/3$ cup evaporated milk

Mix and shape into small meatballs. Bake at 400 degrees F for 12-15 minutes. Drain grease.

SAUCE

2   onion rings
3   tablespoons vinegar
4   tablespoons Worcestershire sauce
1   14-ounce bottle ketchup
1   equal part water
2   teaspoons salt
$1/4$ teaspoon cayenne pepper (use $1/2$ teaspoon for a more spicy flavor)
$1/4$ cup brown sugar
  We like to add a little "sweet" barbecue sauce to taste.

Bring to a boil. Simmer for 15 minutes. Pour over drained meatballs. Put back in oven for 10-15 minutes.

Beaumont
Music, Memories and Museums

In addition to being known for its great food, fabulous music and good times, Beaumont is home to country music stars Tracy Byrd, Mark Chesnutt, Clay Walker and the legendary George Jones.

Beaumont is proud of its hometown music heroes as they rise in stardom and continue to honor the city that gave them their start.

Such a star is Tracy Byrd.

Annually, Byrd shows Southeast Texas how much he loves his old stomping grounds by hosting a three-day, Homecoming Weekend, featuring a concert with Tracy and friends, golf tournament and "Big Bass Tournament." This event is just one way Tracy supports his hometown.

On January 10, 2001, Beaumont paid tribute to the famous oil field, Spindletop, with a 100-year Anniversary Celebration featuring Tracy Byrd, former President George Bush and other local dignitaries. During the celebration, Tracy treated crowds to an original song, "Spindletop," which he wrote for the occasion telling the unforgettable story of the Lucas gusher.

Rich in heritage, history and natural resources, Beaumont has much to offer visitors. All forms of recreational activities, including golf, birding, canoeing, hunting and fresh and saltwater fishing are available. Just a stones throw away is the Gulf of Mexico, the East Texas Lake Country, and the biological crossroads of North America, the Big Thicket National Preserve. There's something here for all tastes.

Beaumont has also been referred to as the museum capital of Texas. Attractions include everything from the world class Texas Energy Museum to the world's largest fire hydrant. One can enjoy entertainment virtually any day of the year, from classical to zydeco, pop and jazz, to Cajun and Country. There are river rides, swamp tours, canoe expeditions and camping – even horse racing and casino gaming in nearby Louisiana. In a word, there is an experience for everyone in Beaumont…the Right Side of Texas.

43

South Texas Plains

South Texas Plains

The Texas South Plains sweep from the historic avenues of San Antonio down across the brush country where cowboys once herded wild cattle and on toward Mexico and the rich, tropical delta of the Lower Rio Grande Valley where palm trees sway in the gulf winds, and the orchards are thick with groves of oranges and grapefruit.

San Antonio is the mirror of diversity. Its river became the lifeline for five Spanish missions that stand even today with the pride and dignity of their heritage. One is the Alamo, a sacred shrine of freedom. The Paseo Del Rio follows the meandering path of the river for three leisurely miles, weaving in and out of tranquil gardens and sidewalk cafes, crafts shops and waterfalls, fountains and night clubs that throb, rock and swing to the pulsating sounds of flamenco brass or happy jazz or even the heartache of country blues.

Antique cottages in La Villita, a 19th century inheritance, house art galleries and crafts shops. The Spanish Governor's Palace has been around since 1749. The Institute of Texan Cultures honors the many different nationalities who came, fought and civilized the land called Texas. San Antonio has its performing and visual arts: musical revues, Broadway plays, ballets, symphony and jazz concerts. The McNay Art Museum showcases the classical works of Cezanne, Van Gogh, Gauguin, Renoir and Picasso. The Museum of Art is noted for its modern, Pre-Columbian and Spanish Colonial Art, as well as Mexican folk art. And outside the city, Six Flags Fiesta rises out of an old barren quarry with rides both calm, wild and even wet. Nearby, Shamu, the personable killer whale, stars at Sea World of Texas, the world's largest marine life park.

The wind-sculptured landscape of Choke Canyon Reservoir at Three Rivers has become one of the region's top recreational areas. Whitetail deer, turkey and javalina dart among the brush. Fishermen explore the shoreline for bass, crappie, bluegill and sunfish. Ranching dominates Kenedy, once known as Six Shooter Junction. Back in the 1870s, cattlemen were rounding up longhorns, collecting them on the prairies around Pleasanton and pushing them up the trails to Kansas. It's little wonder why Pleasanton bills itself as the "Birthplace of the Cowboy."

McAllen is always in bloom. Its palm-tree shaded streets are clustered with bougainvillea, hibiscus and roses. Roadways wind through orange and grapefruit groves, fields of sugar cane and cotton. The region's cultural relationship with Mexico is on display at the McAllen International Museum, an earth science gallery dealing with fossils and dinosaurs that once stalked the valley. An international bridge ties McAllen to the streets of Reynosa, Mexico, a border town offering dining and shopping for jewelry, ceramics, onyx, leather goods, hand-woven fabrics and hand-blown glass in the colorful Pink Zone and Zaragoza Market.

Mercedes refers top itself as the Queen City of the Rio Grande Valley, its farmsteads ripe with melons, carrots, onions, sugar cane and cotton. The ancient chapel of La Lomita at Mission remembers the Oblate priests who rode beneath the palms, bringing with them the gospel and seeds for the first orange groves into the region.

Southwest of Weslaco is the 2,000 acre Santa Ana National Wildlife Refuge, a sanctuary for many species of birds and wildlife, including the endangered jaguarundi and strange chachalaca, something akin to a wild chicken that only lives in the thick brush of the Rio Grande delta. And Laredo possesses the exotic and foreign flavor of its southern neighbor, Mexico

Goliad's Presidio La Bahia

45

San Antonio

A Crossroads of Texas Cultures

Long a crossroads of history and a meeting place of cultures, San Antonio is a rich blend of deeply rooted traditions and twenty-first century cosmopolitan flair, a place where America's past and present merge to create a unique vibrancy.

San Antonio is the Paseo del Rio, an urban masterpiece better known as the "River Walk." With its cobblestone and flagstone paths bordering both sides of the San Antonio River, Twenty feet below street level, the River Walk has multiple personalities—quiet and park-like in some stretches, while other areas are full of activity with European-style sidewalk cafes, specialty boutiques, art galleries, nightclubs and gleaming high-rise hotels.

San Antonio is the Alamo, where, for thirteen days in 1836, a force of 189 defenders fought to the death against some 4,000 Mexican troops. The cry "Remember the Alamo" became the rallying point of the Texan revolution against Mexico. Located in the heart of downtown, the Alamo is a shrine and a museum.

San Antonio is Texas-sized fun at SeaWorld, the world's largest marine life park, and Six Flags Fiesta, the town built just for fun. San Antonio has two impressive museums in the McNay Art Museum, set in a Mediterranean-style mansion, and the San Antonio Museum of Art, which features the Nelson A. Rockefeller Center for Latin American Art. The story of Texas is portrayed in The Institute of Texan Cultures, and near Market Square will be the Smithsonian Museum. San Antonio is shopping from numerous antique shops and malls throughout the city to picturesque La Villita, Market Square and the River Walk in the historic heart of the city.

San Antonio is an array of dining options, from French cuisine to Chinese, Texas steaks, barbecue, Soul Food, Cajun and, of course, Tex-Mex. Many restaurants are open 24 hours a day in case a craving for guacamole or fajitas develops at 3 o'clock in the morning.

Half-Dried Tomato Salsa

Serves 4

9	whole Roma tomatoes, halved
1	teaspoon oregano, chopped
1	teaspoon salt, sea or Kosher
1	teaspoon garlic, chopped
1	small white onion, sliced thin
1	whole Habanero pepper, halved
6	tablespoons olive oil
2	tablespoons cilantro leaves

Rub the tomatoes with a little of the oil, and sprinkle with oregano, garlic and salt. Place on a baking sheet, cut side up, and set in a 200 degree F-oven for about 1 to 1 $\frac{1}{2}$ hours until tomatoes are semi-dry. In a skillet, heat the oil over medium heat, and fry the onion until golden. Remove the onion, and chop with the tomatoes. Return to the oil with the Habanero pepper, and gently simmer for 10 minutes. Remove the Habanero pepper, and finish with cilantro leaves.

The Alamo ... A mission, a fortress, a shrine

46

Terrific Tostadas

Serves 4-6.

1 (16-ounce) can refried beans
4-6 beef patties
1 onion, sliced
1 package corn tortillas

Optional Topping:

Lettuce, chopped
Tomatoes, chopped
Sour cream
Monterey Jack and/or cheddar cheese
Salsa

Heat beans. Cook patties on one side, then add sliced onions and cook both until patties are done. Heat tortillas. Put pattie on a tortilla, cover with beans and top with onions. Add choice of toppings.

Hot Tamale Soup

Serves 6-8.

1 pound ground chuck
$\frac{1}{2}$ cup chopped onion
$\frac{1}{2}$ cup chopped bell pepper
1 teaspoon chili powder
1 teaspoon ground cumin
3 (14.5-ounce) cans beef broth
1 (10-ounce) package frozen corn
1 (15-ounce) can Mexican beans
12 tamales, shucks removed, sliced

Brown ground chuck with onion and bell pepper. Add remaining ingredients. Simmer 30 minutes, then add tamales. Heat thoroughly and serve.

Chilled Mexican Mayan Gulf Shrimp with Crispy Plantains and Roasted Corn Huitlacoche Salsa

Executive Chef Scott Cohen, La Mansion Del Rio Hotel, San Antonio
Serves 6-8

Roasted Corn Huitlacoche Salsa

5 ears of corn, roasted
2 tablespoons garlic, roasted
1 bunch cilantro leaves
1 serrano pepper
1 (7-ounce) can huitlacoche (may be purchased in Spanish stores)
2 ounces fresh lime juice
   Olive oil
   Onion powder, cumin and salt to taste

Roast garlic and lightly char corn on a grill. Cut corn off the cob. Put all ingredients in a food processor bowl, and pulse until chunky. Season to taste.

NOTE: If too thick, thin out with water.

Lemon Sour Cream

1 cup sour cream
2 lemons, juiced
   Salt and pepper to taste

Place sour cream in a mixing bowl, and mix with lemon juice. Season with salt and pepper.

Main Dish

16-20 shrimp, peeled and poached
16 ounces huitlacoche salsa
4 tablespoon lemon sour cream
4 sprig cilantro leaf
12 plantain chips

For plantain chips, slice a banana into chips that are paper thin, and fry at 300 degrees F until crispy.

Use an oversized margarita or martini glass to serve each individual. Place 4 ounces of salsa in glass over 3-5 shrimp, surrounded by 3 plantain chips. Swirl one tablespoon of sour cream in the middle, and garnish with fresh cilantro.

48

Mexican Bean Soup

Serves 4-5.

4   slices bacon, diced
$3/4$ cup onion, chopped
$3/4$ cup celery, chopped
1   clove garlic, minced
1   (4-ounce) can green chilies
1   (16-ounce) can refried beans
$1/4$ teaspoon black pepper
$1/4$ teaspoon chili powder
     Several dashes of hot pepper sauce
1   (13 $1/2$-ounce) can chicken broth
     Cheddar cheese, shredded
     Tortilla chips, broken

In a 2-quart saucepan, cook bacon until crisp. Add onion, celery and garlic. Cover and cook over low heat, stirring occasionally, for 10 minutes, or until vegetables are tender but not brown. Add green chilies, beans, pepper, chili powder and hot pepper sauce. Stir in chicken broth. Bring to a boil. Serve in bowls; sprinkle cheese and tortilla chips over each serving.

Microwave:

In a 2-quart microwave-safe casserole, microwave bacon on HIGH for 3-5 minutes or until crisp. Add onion, celery and garlic; cover and microwave at 50 percent power for 5 minutes, or until vegetables are tender, stirring occasionally. Add green chilies, beans, pepper, chili powder and hot pepper sauce. Stir in chicken broth. Microwave on HIGH for 5-6 minutes, or until soup boils. Proceed as directed above to serve.

Chilies Stuffed With Texas Chevre Goat Cheese And Sun-Dried Tomatoes

Serves 8.

8   fresh chilies, roasted and left whole
$1/2$ pound goat cheese
2   ounces cream cheese, softened
8   red bell peppers, roasted
$1/4$ cup olive oil
$1/2$ teaspoon salt
1   tablespoon sugar, or to taste
1   tablespoon balsamic Vinegar
$1/2$ cup sun-dried tomatoes packed in olive oil, drained and chopped fine

Peel the chilies carefully (wear rubber gloves), leaving them whole, slit them lengthwise, and discard the seeds. In a food processor, puree the goat cheese with cream cheese, transfer the mixture to a bowl and chill it until firm. In the cleaned food processor, puree the bell peppers with the oil, salt, sugar and vinegar for 3-4 minutes, or until mixture is smooth. Transfer the sauce to a bowl, and chill, covered, for 1 hour. Arrange the chilies on a work surface, and lay them open flat. Fill each chili with about 2 tablespoons of the cheese mixture. With a knife make a $3/8$-inch canal in the cheese mixture. Fill canals with 2 teaspoons of tomatoes, and press the chili and the cheese mixture around the tomatoes to enclose them. Transfer the stuffed chilies as they are made to a plate, cover and chill them for 2 hours. Divide the sauce evenly on 8 serving plates. Cut each chili with a serrated knife into 5-6 slices, and lay on top of sauce on each plate.

San Antonio Style Chicken Wings

Makes 24 appetizers.

12   chicken wings
1   cup picante sauce
$1/3$ cup catsup
$1/4$ cup honey
$1/4$ teaspoon ground cumin
$2/3$ cup sour cream

Cut wings in half at joints; discard wing tips. Combine $1/3$ cup of the picante sauce, catsup, honey and cumin; pour over chicken. Place in refrigerator; marinate at least 1 hour, turning once. Drain chicken, reserving marinade. Place on rack of foil-lined broiler pan. Bake at 375 degrees F for 30 minutes. Brush chicken with reserved marinade: turn and bake, brushing generously with marinade every 10 minutes until tender, about 30 minutes. Place 6 inches from heat in preheated broiler; broil 2-3 minutes, or until sauce looks dry. Turn, broil 2-3 minutes, or until sauce looks dry. Spoon sour cream into small clear glass bowl; top with remaining $2/3$ cup picante sauce. Serve with chicken.

Easy Chili Rellenos

Makes 12 servings.

$1/4$	pound lean ground beef
1	onion, chopped
1	clove garlic, chopped
	Salt to taste
	Pepper to taste
$1/4$	teaspoon cumino
2	cups shredded cheddar cheese
2	cups cooked rice
12	large fresh poblano peppers, roasted and peeled
12	egg roll wrappers
	Oil to deep fry

Brown ground beef. Drain drippings; add onion, garlic, salt pepper and cumin. Cook, stirring often until onions are golden brown. Remove from heat; add cheese and cooked rice, stirring to blend. Split peppers lengthwise, remove seeds and pat dry. Stuff with meat mixture. Place each filled pepper diagonally on an egg roll wrapper. Bring lower rectangle point over pepper, and tuck under. Place right side over center, bring top point down over pepper and then roll to left side. Seal edges with few drops of water. Deep fry at 325 degrees F.

Guacamole Salad

Serves 4.

	Shredded lettuce
4	tostada shells
2	ripe avocados, peeled, pitted and mashed
$1/2$	cup chunky salsa
2	tablespoons finely chopped onion
1	tablespoons lemon juice
$1/2$	teaspoon salt
$1/4$	teaspoon garlic powder

Preheat oven to 350 degrees F. Heat shells 5-7 minutes. Line cooled shells with shredded lettuce. Combine remaining ingredients, and spoon approximately $1/2$ cup of guacamole into each shell. Garnish with additional shredded lettuce. Break off portions of shell to use for dipping.

Mexican Garden Salad

Serves 4-6

1 cup sour cream	
1	(16-ounce) jar salsa, divided usage
3	cups cooked and shredded chicken
$1/4$	cup water (omit for microwave preparation)
1	(1 $1/4$-ounce) package taco seasoning mix
1	head lettuce, torn in bite-size pieces
3	cups broccoli florettes
1	small red onion, sliced thin and separated into rings
1	avocado, peeled, pitted and chopped
1	carrot, shredded
1	large tomato, chopped
1	(4-ounce) can chopped green chilies, drained
1	(4-ounce) cup shredded cheddar cheese
1	(7 $1/2$-ounce) box tortilla chips, broken

Combine 1 cup salsa and sour cream; refrigerate until ready to serve. In a large skillet, combine chicken, remaining salsa, water and taco seasoning mix. Bring to a boil, and let simmer 15-20 minutes. In a large serving bowl, layer vegetables. Top with chicken mixture, chilies and cheese. Toss to combine. Top each salad with broken tortilla chips and salsa and sour cream dressing.

Mexican Steak Ranchero

Serves 4-6.

2	pounds round steak
1	teaspoon olive oil
1	large onion, sliced
1	garlic clove, mashed
1	(16-ounce) can sliced mushrooms
4	tablespoons butter
1	cup beef bouillon
1	(8-ounce) jar picante sauce
$1/2$	cup white wine, optional
2	cups cooked long grain rice
	Salt and pepper to taste

Cut steaks into individual servings. Brown in oil; in heavy skillet, sauté onions, garlic and mushrooms in butter, just until onion becomes soft. Add bouillon, picante sauce and meat. Cover and allow to simmer about 1 hour. Add wine the last 10 minutes of the cooking time. Serve over rice.

The whales visit for lunch at Sea World

Sea World
Dine With Shamu

San Antonio offers two memorable outdoor dining locales – the famed San Antonio River Walk, or Paseo del Rio, and SeaWorld San Antonio's Shamu Stadium.

Shamu Stadium? That's right! It's the site of Dine With Shamu, an unforgettable buffet served backstage and poolside at the multi-million-gallon home for world-famous Shamu and companion killer whales. While enjoying delicious cuisine, SeaWorld guests get a close-up look at the awesome whales, an opportunity to meet animal trainers and ask questions, as well as have a tidal wave of great photo opportunities.

One of the highlights of Dine With Shamu is the scrumptious carrot cake expertly prepared by SeaWorld's culinary staff. The recipe appears on the opposite page.

Dine With Shamu is offered on selected dates during SeaWorld San Antonio's operating season. For more information and reservations, call (210)523-3900.

SeaWorld San Antonio Carrot Cake

Serves 8

Cake:

1	cup chopped dates
2	cups granulated sugar
1 $\frac{1}{4}$	cups salad oil
1	teaspoon salt
4	eggs
2	cups all-purpose flour
1	teaspoon baking powder
1	teaspoon baking soda
8	ounces crushed pineapple
2	teaspoons ground cinnamon
3	cups chopped carrots
$\frac{2}{3}$	cup raisins
1	teaspoon vanilla extract
1	cup pecan pieces

Preheat oven to 350 degrees F. Add dates and sugar; mix for one minute. Continue mixing and slowly add salt, salad oil and then eggs. Add flour, baking powder and baking soda; mix until smooth. Pour into two greased 9-inch pans – $\frac{3}{4}$ full. Bake at 350 degrees F for 40-50 minutes, or until top of cake springs back when lightly touched with hand.

Cream Cheese Icing:

1	pound cream cheese
5	ounces butter
1	pound powdered sugar
	Vanilla flavor to taste
	Almond extract to taste

Mix softened butter with cream cheese; mix until smooth. Add powdered sugar, and mix until smooth…scraping bowl at least twice. Add both vanilla and almond extracts; again, mix until smooth.
continued on next page

Preparations:

To toast almonds, place almonds in a single layer on a paper lined sheet pan. Bake at 350 degrees F for 10-12 minutes, or until lightly browned. Use two cake rounds per cake. Cut both rounds in half. Therefore, there will be four layers per cake. Lay one $1/2$-layer on serving plate. Frost top of only first layer. Repeat for next three layers. Cover top of cake with icing. Avoid getting icing on the side of cake. Melt currant jelly, and brush on sides of cake. Place toasted almonds on side. Keep refrigerated until ready to serve.

Assembly:

Carrot cake rounds
Currant jelly
Almonds, sliced and toasted
Cream cheese icing

Traditional Cheese Enchiladas

Serves 8-10.

$1/2$	tablespoon chili pepper
1	tablespoon paprika
2	cloves garlic, chopped
$1/4$	teaspoon camino
$1/2$	cup flour
$1/4$	tablespoon oregano
1	quart chicken broth
$1/4$	tablespoon salt, or to taste
$3/8$	cup oil
$3/4$	pound cheddar cheese, grated
$3/4$	pound Monterey Jack cheese, grated
1	onion, chopped
	Additional oil
2	dozen tortillas (red tortillas are traditional)

Sauce:

If using ancho chilies, remove stems and seeds from pods, simmer in hot water until skin loosens and put through sieve to separate the skin from chili pulp. Fry the paprika, camino and garlic in $3/8$ cup oil for 1 minute. Add the flour, and cook until just brown. Add the chili pulp or chili pepper, the oregano and the chicken broth, bring to a boil and simmer until thick.

To Assemble Enchiladas:

Mix the 2 kinds of cheese and the chopped onion. Heat $1/4$ inch of oil in a pan. With tongs, dip tortillas briefly in the hot oil until soft. Put 1 tablespoon of the sauce in the tortilla, stuff with cheese and onions, roll up and place side by side in baking or microwave pan. Stuff all of the tortillas. Sprinkle top with cheese, onions and sauce. Bake in 425 degree F-oven, or microwave until cheese is melted.

Speedy Fajita Salad

Makes 6 servings.

1	cup picante sauce
2	green onions with tops, thinly sliced
$1/4$	cup chopped fresh cilantro
$1/4$	cup vegetable oil
1	teaspoon lemon juice
1	clove garlic, minced
$1/2$	teaspoon salt
1	(15-ounce) can pinto beans, drained
2	medium tomatoes, seeded and diced
1	ripe avocado, peeled, seeded and diced
1	pound beef sirloin or top round steak
	Salt and pepper
4	cups shredded lettuce
12	flour tortillas, heated

Combine first 7 ingredients; mix well. Toss beans with $1/4$ cup of the picante mixture; chill. Toss tomatoes and avocado with $1/4$ cup of the picante mixture; chill. Sprinkle meat with salt and pepper; broil, grill or fry to desired doneness. Slice thinly across the grain; toss with $1/4$ cup of the picante mixture; arrange on platter. Arrange beans, tomato mixture and meat on greens. Serve with tortillas, and add additional picante sauce.

Tamale Pie

Serves 6-8.

2	pounds ground beef
2	packages taco seasoning
$1 1/2$	teaspoons ground jalapeno powder, divided
2	(6-ounce) packages cornbread mix
2	(15-ounce) cans pinto or Mexican beans
2	(17-ounce) cans corn, drained
2	(8-ounce) cans tomato sauce
2	cups water

Preheat oven to 400 degrees F. Brown hamburger meat. Add taco seasoning and $1/2$ teaspoon jalapeno powder; heat 5 minutes. In a mixing bowl, combine cornbread mix and 1 teaspoon jalapeno powder. In a 9 x 13-inch baking dish, combine beans, corn, tomato sauce and hamburger mixture. Cover with cornbread mixture. Carefully cover cornbread mixture with water, trying not to pour a hole through the cornbread. Bake 1 hour.

Black Bean and Goat Cheese Enchiladas

Serves 4.

$3/4$ cup chicken broth, divided
4-5 tomatillos (husk removed), rinsed and chopped (or substitute green tomatoes, canned or fresh)
3 cloves garlic, peeled and divided
$1/2$ cup chopped yellow onion
2 serrano chilies, stemmed and seeded
1 tablespoon cilantro, chopped
1 cup cooked black beans
4 tablespoons fresh mango or papaya, diced
2 scallions, white part only, thinly sliced
$1/4$ cup (about 2 ounces) goat cheese
Salt to taste
$1/4$ cup corn oil
4 corn tortillas (6-inch size)
Red yellow bell peppers, cut in thin strips, to garnish

To make salsa: in medium-size saucepan, cook $1/2$ cup chicken broth, tomatillos, 2 cloves garlic, onion and 1 serrano chili over medium-high heat for 10 minutes, stirring often. Place mixture in blender with cilantro, and puree until smooth. Reserve salsa. Mince remaining garlic and serrano chilies. In a medium saucepan, place black beans, remaining $1/4$ cup broth, minced garlic and serrano chilies, mango or papaya and scallions. Bring to a boil, and whisk in goat cheese. Season with salt, remove from heat, and keep warm. In a medium-size skillet, heat the corn oil until just smoking. Pass each tortilla through the oil to moisten and seal. Place between paper towels to drain. To assemble, place $1/4$ of the bean and goat cheese mixture down the center of each tortilla. Roll tortillas and place seam-side down on plates. Spoon the salsa equally over the filled tortillas, and sprinkle with red and/or yellow pepper strips.

Old San Antonio Fajitas

Serves 2-3.

2 pounds skirt or flank steak
Fajita seasoning
1 cup oil
1/4 cup salsa
2 cloves fresh garlic, smashed
2 limes, juiced
4-6 flour tortillas, warmed
Picante sauce
Guacamole
1 onion, chopped (optional)

Rub steak with fajita seasoning. Combine oil, salsa, garlic and lime juice. Marinate meat for 6-8 hours in the salsa mixture. Cook outside over charcoal, or bake in oven for 3 hours at 275 degrees F. Cut into strips, and serve in hot flour tortillas with picante sauce, guacamole and onion.

Peachy Surprise Salad

Serves 6-8.

$3/4$ cup butter, melted
2 $1/4$ cups crushed pretzels
1 $3/4$ cups sugar
2 (8-ounce) packages cream cheese, softened
1 large (16-ounce) carton whipped topping
3 cups sliced peaches
1 (15 $1/2$-ounce) can pineapple chunks
1 (6-ounce) package peach gelatin
Pecans to garnish

Combine butter, pretzels and $1/4$ cup sugar in 13 x 9-inch pan, mixing and spreading over bottom of pan. Blend cream cheese, whipped toppings and 1 $1/2$ cups sugar in a bowl. Spread over pretzel layer. Drain juices from peaches and pineapples, reserving juices. Combine with enough water to measure 2 cups, and heat to boiling. Dissolve gelatin in hot juice mixture. Stir in 2 cups ice; chill until thickened. Fold in fruit. Spread over cream cheese mixture. Garnish with pecans.

Texas Traditional Pecan Pie

Serves 6-8.

3 tablespoons butter
1 teaspoon vanilla
$3/4$ cup granulated sugar
3 eggs, well beaten
$1/2$ cup pecan pieces
1 cup dark corn syrup
$1/8$ teaspoon salt
$3/4$ cup pecan halves
1 (9-inch) pie crust shell, unbaked

Cream butter with vanilla, gradually adding sugar. Add eggs in thirds, creaming well after each addition. Thoroughly blend in pecan pieces along with syrup and salt. Turn into unbaked pastry shell. Bake at 450 degrees F for 10 minutes, then reduce heat to 350 degrees F. Arrange pecan halves to cover top of filling. Continue baking 30-35 minutes until set. Cool before serving.

Pasta with Yellow Squash, Sun-Dried Tomatoes and Fresh Ricotta

Serves 4-6

2 pounds yellow squash, sliced
1 small onion, sliced
1 clove garlic, minced
$1/4$ cup extra virgin olive oil
$1/4$-$1/2$ pound sun-dried tomatoes, sliced into strips
1 pound dried pasta
    Water and salt to cook pasta
1 pound ricotta
    Small bunch fresh basil leaves
$1/4$ pound grated cheese

Sauté squash with onion and garlic in olive oil until slightly limp. Cut tomatoes into narrow strips. Cook pasta in rapidly boiling, salted water until al dente, and drain. Toss pasts with ricotta, then add vegetables, tomatoes and fresh basil leaves, and toss briefly. Sprinkle with grated cheese. Toss again briefly.

Chicken/Spinach Sour Cream Enchiladas

Serves 6-8

1 chicken, whole
1 onion, chopped
2 cloves garlic, minced
    Dash cumin
    Dash coriander
1 (12-ounce) package fresh spinach
2 teaspoons white vinegar
12 corn tortillas
1 (16-ounce) can sour cream
1 pound Monterey Jack cheese, grated
    Paprika
    Sliced jalapenos

Boil chicken with onion, garlic, cumin and coriander 2 hours, remove bone, retain broth. Cook spinach 30 minutes with vinegar; strain. Mix chicken and spinach; chop finely. Dip tortillas, one at a time, into hot chicken broth, then roll chicken/spinach mixture in tortilla 1 $1/2$-inches thick. Place flap down in enchilada dish. Gently beat sour cream with 2 tablespoons chicken broth until creamy. Pour over enchiladas. Heat in oven 350 degrees F for 30 minutes. Garnish with cheese, paprika and sliced jalapenos.

Herb N' Wine Muffins

Makes 12 muffins

2 cups biscuit mix
$1/4$ cup chopped green onion
1 tablespoon sugar
1 teaspoon each fresh dill, basil, oregano
1 egg
$1/2$ cup milk
4 ounces cheddar cheese, shredded
$1/4$ cup butter
$1/4$ cup white wine

Combine biscuit mix, onion, sugar and herbs. Mix the egg and milk together; beat slightly. Add this, 2/3rds of the cheese, the butter and wine to the dry ingredients. Beat until blended. Turn out into a well-greased muffin tin. Sprinkle the remaining cheese on top. Bake at 400 degrees F until brown and crusty, about 15 minutes. Serve with butter.

Moon over McAllen

McAllen

The Flavor of Mexico, Served Up Texas Style

Imagine a city warmed by sub tropical breezes and complemented by the spicy charms of Historic Old Mexico. Now imagine all that served up on a Texas platter overflowing with a smorgasbord of outdoor pleasures year round. McAllen is just that. Nestled in the heart of Texas' southernmost region, the Rio Grande Valley, McAllen is just a country dance step from Mexico's front door and the lovely resort beaches of South Padre Island. And, because the area is as far south as the tip of Florida, the weather is ideal, even in the dead of winter, for outdoor sport and recreation.

The Rio Grande Valley is the best birding location in the U.S., and several fine golf courses are open year round with very reasonable green fees. The McAllen area is famous for fishing on both sides of the border. McAllen is also the Square Dance Capital of the World.

American and Continental offer jet flights daily to McAllen International Airport. And Aerolitoral Airlines has service to Monterrey, Mexico.

McAllen is a true bi-national destination. It has a flavor all its own – tangy and delightful – that tantalizes the senses while soothing the spirit. It is worth a visit.

Grapefruit Marmalade

Yields 5 to 8 pints

20 Texas Ruby Star grapefruits
8   cups granulated sugar

Thoroughly wash grapefruit. Peel grapefruit rind with a stripper, saving the fruit. Chop peeled rind into small pieces, and place in a pan of water. Boil peeling for 5 minutes. Drain and repeat boiling process another 5 minutes. Juice grapefruit and remove seeds. Measure juice, pulp and rind, and place into a stainless steel pan. Add an equal amount of sugar, and stir. Let stand covered overnight. Place kettle of marmalade ingredients on stovetop, and boil for 30 minutes or to jelling point. Remove from heat.

Fill sterilized jars with cooked marmalade to $1/4$ inch from top, and seal. Bring kettle of water to boil, and immerse sealed jars; boil for 10 minutes. Remove and thoroughly cool before labeling.

55

Panhandle Plains

Panhandle Plains

The Panhandle Plains of Texas capture the mythical spirit of the Old West. Ranchers chased out buffalo and replaced them with cattle. Its terrain was blackened and stained with oil. Men of the soil learned how to irrigate the earth, and great farms spread across the Staked Plains. And brave new towns grew up on a prairie where the sweat of those cowboys, roughnecks and farmers touched the ground.

Amarillo has long been the economic backbone of the Texas Panhandle. The oil boom exploded across the high plains, and fortunes were made overnight, changing the face and future of Amarillo. A winery toasts the good life, and towering over the plains is a steel Helium Monument, signifying that the region provides ninety percent of the world's helium supply. Cowboy paintings and sculpture at the Amarillo Art Center portray the beauty and bravery of the Southwest. And working ranches in the area offer demonstrations of roping and branding, dinners at sundown and horse-drawn wagon trips out across the Llano Estacado and toward Palo Duro Canyon for authentic cowboy breakfasts.

When Coronado searched for lost cities of gold in 1541, he found instead the cliffs of Palo Duro, plunging 800 feet off the edge of those table-topped plains, a vermilion gorge torn open by the waters of the Red River. It cuts and slashes its way for 120 miles, forming the largest state park in Texas, covering 15,103 acres. The high plains are flat, void of trees, but on the canyon floor are mesquite, juniper and cottonwoods, all clustering together along the creek bank. Sagebrush casts its silver sheen in moonlight. Yucca leaps from the ground like living daggers. And deer, fox, badger, beaver and aoudad sheep roam the rocky bluffs. During the summer months, the outdoor drama TEXAS is presented in Palo Duro Canyon's Pioneer Amphitheater.

A vivid portrait of the region is tucked away in Canyon's Panhandle Plains Historical Museum. A wooden sidewalk leads through Pioneer Town, lined with shops and stores and a school that showcase a small community in the 1880s. Lubbock's Ranching Heritage Center is a collection of buildings salvaged from homesteads and cattle operations whose names have become legendary: the XIT, Four Sixes, Matador,

The lighthouse in Palo Duro Canyon

Panhandle Plains

JA and Waggoner Ranches. The center is located atop the caprock escarpment, which once formed a natural border lying between farmlands and livestock pastures.

In San Angelo, Fort Concho looks as stern as it did in the 1870s when blue-coated soldiers were riding across the West Texas prairies, protecting settlers, guarding mail and stage routes and exploring new territory. Living history units now patrol the ground, marching in close order and riding in cavalry drills around the twenty-one limestone buildings of the old outpost. Concho Street, which originally linked the fort to the trading post, is lined with historical buildings, including a general store, working saddle shop, antique and brass shops and a genuine turn-of-the-twentieth century bordello museum. Miss Hattie's became the most elegant business in town with pressed tin ceilings, gilded in gold; ornate iron brass and oak beds with velvet and satin spreads; oriental rugs and the first indoor plumbing in San Angelo.

Abilene also clings to vestiges of its early days. Fort Phantom Hill rises ghost-like in jagged columns from the prairie floor. About all that's left are a couple of stone buildings and a few rock chimneys that stood so proud alongside the Butterfield Trail. Buffalo Gap is a collection of antique buildings more than a century old, including the original Taylor County courthouse and jail. Abilene's Grace Cultural Center, housing art and historical museums both, was resurrected from the remains of the old Grace Hotel, a gracious reminder of 1909.

Down the road, Cisco has Conrad Hilton's first hotel, bought during the glory days of the oil boom. Hilton always referred to the old Mobley Hotel as a "cross between a flophouse and a gold mine." Eastland fondly remembers "Old Rip," the famed crusty, old horned toad that was placed in the cornerstone of its new courthouse in 1897. Lo and behold, he was still breathing when the cornerstone was opened thirty-one years later. "Old Rip" promptly toured the country and even paid a somewhat dignified visit to President Calvin Coolidge. Coleman calls itself the "Hunting Capital of Texas." Stamford has its Texas Cowboy Reunion and Roundup Rodeo, and Sweetwater holds the world's largest rattlesnake roundup.

A bouquet of high plains color

58

Amarillo

A Western Portrait

Amarillo is the heart of Texas' ranching industry. Drive in any direction, and you'll find cowboys and cowgirls riding horseback, tending large herds of cattle. From cowboys to canyons, big steaks to big sky, come to Amarillo to step into the Real Texas.

Visit Amarillo to see Palo Duro Canyon, one of the largest canyons in the nation; the Panhandle-Plains Historical Museum, the Smithsonian of Texas; the American Quarter Horse Museum, a tribute to the most popular equine breed in the nation; the outdoor musical drama TEXAS, held each summer in Palo Duro Canyon State Park; and the Big Texan Steak Ranch, home to the world famous 72 oz. steak (it's free if you can eat the entire dinner in an hour).

And remember, the cowboy you meet is likely to be the real deal.

Above the Amarillo High Country

Peppered Rib Eye Steak

Submitted by Jeff Frazer and Molly Ann Forbes of Amarillo, Texas
Serves 8

4	beef rib eye steaks (1 $1/2$ inches thick)
1	tablespoon olive oil
1	tablespoon garlic powder
1	tablespoon paprika
2	teaspoons dried ground oregano
2	teaspoons dried ground thyme
1 $1/2$	teaspoons pepper
1	teaspoon salt
1	teaspoon lemon pepper
1	teaspoon ground red pepper
	Orange slices (optional)
	Parsley springs (optional)

Brush steaks lightly with olive oil. In a small bowl, combine all seasonings. Sprinkle seasonings over steaks, and press into both sides. Cover and chill for 1 hour. Grill steaks, turning once, over medium-hot coals. Grill 14-18 minutes for rare; 18-22 minutes for medium; 24-28 minutes for well-done. Place on warm serving platter; cut across grain into thick slices. Garnish with orange slices and parsley.

Honey Cheese Cake

Serves 6-8.

1   (3-ounce) package lemon gelatin
$1/2$ cup boiling water
8   ounces cream cheese
$1/2$ cup honey
2   teaspoons lemon juice
1   teaspoon vanilla
1 $1/2$ cups evaporated milk, chilled
1   (9-inch) graham cracker pie shell

Mix gelatin with boiling water. Cool. Do not let set. Mix cream cheese with honey, lemon juice and vanilla. Whip chilled milk. Fold into cream cheese mixture. Pour into pie shell.

Pepper Relish Surprise Corn Muffins

Makes 12 muffins.

1   cup cornmeal
1   cup flour
$1/4$ cup sugar
4   teaspoons baking powder
$1/2$ teaspoon salt
1   cup milk
1   egg
$1/4$ cup vegetable oil
$1/2$ cup sweet pepper relish

In a medium bowl, combine cornmeal, flour, sugar, baking powder and salt. Combine milk, egg and oil. Add to dry ingredients, mixing just until dry ingredients are moistened. Fill greased, medium-size muffin cups $2/3$ full of cornmeal mixture. Place 1 $1/2$ teaspoons relish in center of each muffin cup; press lightly into batter. Bake at 425 degrees F for 15-20 minutes. Cool 5 minutes in muffin pans; remove to wire cooling rack.

Tangy Bean Soup

Serves 10.

1   pound dried beans (black, pinto or kidney)
8   cups no-salt beef broth, plus enough water
        to cover
1   large onion, chopped
2   cloves garlic, minced
$1/4$ cup chopped green pepper
$1/4$ cup chopped celery
$1/2$ cup shredded carrots
2   minced jalapenos, optional
1   tablespoon dried parsley
1   tablespoon dried cilantro
$1/4$ teaspoon paprika
$1/4$ teaspoon black pepper
1-2   bay leaves
1   tablespoon low-sodium soy sauce
$1/2$ cup French salad dressing

Wash beans, and soak overnight; drain and rinse. Add to beans all ingredients except soy sauce and dressing. Bring to a boil, reduce heat and simmer for 1 hour. Add more water if needed, plus soy sauce and dressing. Simmer for another hour, or until beans are tender. Discard bay leaves.

Texas Style Barbecue Sauce

Makes 2 cups sauce.

1   cup catsup
4   tablespoons herbal vinegar
4   tablespoons Worcestershire sauce
1   teaspoon prepared mustard
1   cup water
2   tablespoons barbecue seasoning
1   tablespoon brown sugar
2   tablespoons butter or margarine
$1/2$ teaspoon salt
2   teaspoons chopped onion
2   tablespoons lemon juice
1   tablespoon liquid smoke
      Dash of hot pepper sauce

Combine all ingredients in a saucepan, and simmer over low heat for 15 minutes. Use as a basting or dipping sauce with chicken, pork or beef. Place meat in refrigerator overnight for maximum flavor enhancement.

Pecan Crusted Lamb Loin

San Angelo is the sheep and wool capital of America. The lamb is raised on the ranches and processed in San Angelo. This recipe was created by well-known Chef Guy Calluad. The pecans used in the crust are also grown in the San Angelo area.

Serves 4

1 double lamb loin
Debone and reserve the bones for the stock

Lamb Stock:

$1 \frac{1}{2}$ quarts water
1 medium-size yellow onion, coarsely chopped
1 carrot, coarsely chopped
1 celery stalk, coarsely chopped
1 tablespoon tomato paste
1 bay leaf
$\frac{1}{2}$ teaspoon thyme
Salt and pepper to taste

Place water to boil in a medium-size saucepot. In large sauté pan, over high fire, sauté the bones and vegetables until browned: add tomato paste, bay leaf and thyme. Mix well with wooden spoon, and cook for a couple of minutes. Deglaze with a little of the boiling water, and pour into the saucepot with boiling water. Simmer for 1 1/2 hours. Strain the stock into another pot, and chill. When cold, remove the fat that hardened on top.

NOTE: Start sautéing the bones in a dry sauté pan because lamb is very greasy.

1 double lamb loin, split lengthwise
1 tablespoon mild mustard
1 tablespoon molasses
$\frac{1}{2}$ pound crushed fresh pecans
1 teaspoon crushed black pepper
Salt and pepper to taste
1 tablespoon fresh shallots, chopped
1 tablespoon fresh chives, chopped
1 tablespoon fresh chervil, chopped
8 ounces lamb stock
3 tablespoons unsalted butter

In a small bowl, mix mustard, molasses, cracked pepper and pecans. Sprinkle salt and pepper over lamb loins. Heat oven to 350 degrees F. Put a sauté pan (that will fit your oven) over high fire. When hot, sear the lamb on all sides until brown. Remove from fire.

When cooked, spread pecan mixture over lamb, and place back in the sauté pan. Put the sauté pan in hot oven. Bake for 15 minutes. Remove from oven. Place lamb on serving dish. Put 1 tablespoon of butter in the cooking sauté pan. Add shallots and melt until color changes to clear white (do not brown). Add fresh herbs and 8 ounces of stock; bring to a boil. Reduce fire to simmer for 2 minutes, and add remaining butter while stirring sauce constantly. Pour over lamb, and serve.

Ranch Style Brisket

Serves 8-10

1 large beef brisket, trimmed
3 bottles hickory liquid smoke

Pierce several holes in brisket with fork. Place the brisket in a plastic bag, and add bottles of liquid smoke. Tie end of bag, and place in sink to marinate for 3-12 hours, or overnight. When ready to cook, remove brisket from bag, and place in cooling pan fat side up. Place the pan holding brisket on the middle rack of oven at a temperature consistent with desired cooking time: 275 degrees F for 6 hours is perfect. Cook until tender, and it slices easily.

Baked Chili Rellenos

Wonderful complement dish to fajitas or other Mexican food. • Serves 8

1 pound canned green chilies (may use chopped or whole)
1 pound grated Monterey Jack cheese
2 cups milk
$\frac{1}{2}$ cup flour
2 eggs, beaten
1 teaspoon

Mix flour, milk, eggs and salt. Lay chilies in buttered casserole. Add grated cheese. Continue layering as needed. Pour liquid mix over chilies and cheese. Do not cover. Bake 45 minutes to 1 hour in 325 degree F-oven

San Angelo Cooking

Photo Courtesy San Angelo–Standard Times

San Angelo
A Proud Heritage

San Angelo was a frontier fort town, settled after the War Between the States. As part of the Texas Forts Trail, Fort Concho stands today as the best preserved frontier outpost in the West. It is a splendid example of a time when the settlers built their homesteads and ranches on the vastness of a West Texas landscape that was ruled by Native American tribes.

San Angelo is proud of its heritage, which is conserved in the historic city center, Concho Avenue, along with "Miss Hattie's" Bordello Museum, the legendary Concho Pearl, the Cactus Hotel, Santa Fe Depot, The Fine Arts Museum and San Angelo State Park with its buffalo and longhorn herds.

Most cities in Texas have a strong Tex-Mex heritage. And each region demonstrates a subtle difference in the way this traditional cuisine is prepared. The Fuentes Cafe, one of the oldest restaurants in San Angelo created the following traditional recipes— San Angelo style.

Pork Asado in Tomatillo Sauce

Serves 24

10-15	pounds pork meat, cut up like stew meat
1	pound tomatillos
$3/4$	pound chili pods
2	tablespoons salt
2	tablespoons granulated garlic
3	tablespoons flour
1	tablespoon oregano

Rinse pork and place in large stew plot. Cover with water, and simmer until thoroughly cooked, about $1 1/2$ hours. While pork stews, prepare tomatillo sauce. Place tomatillos and chili pepper pods in separate pans. Cover each with water; bring each to a boil. Reduce heat and cook until tender. Remove seeds from chili pepper pods. Add in tomatillos, salt, flour and oregano; mix well. Pour tomatillo sauce over cooked pork meat; stir well. Simmer gently for 20 minutes.

Mexican Rice

Serves 24

8	cups rice, uncooked
9	tablespoons vegetable oil
12	($10 1/2$-ounce) cans chicken broth
2	large onions, finely chopped
3	green bell peppers, seeded and chopped
3	tomatoes, chopped
$2 1/2$	teaspoons salt
2	teaspoons cumin
2	teaspoons granulated garlic

Heat oil in large pot. Sauté rice, onions and bell pepper in hot oil. Stir in remaining ingredients. Bring to a boil. Cover and reduce temperature. Simmer until rice is tender and liquid is absorbed, approximately 25-30 minutes.

63

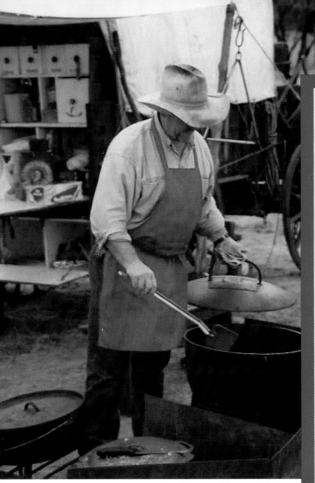

Cowboy cooking in Abilene

Abilene
A Western Heritage

Some may think the West begins some 150 miles east, but the spirit of the American cowboy lives and breathes each day in Abilene. Yet, this thriving city's pioneer past is synchronized to the vibrant, diverse cultural landscape of today. Where else can you greet the morning on horseback with a chuckwagon breakfast and later watch the sunset over the Great Plains to the sounds of a philharmonic orchestra?

Abilene parades its heritage in a collection of venues designed to both educate and entertain. From reliving life-on-the-prairie at Buffalo Gap Historic Village to haunting the ruins of Fort Phantom Hill, visitors can immerse themselves in the history of the Old West and experience firsthand the working ranch life that generations remember. The city's annual Western Heritage Classic draws thousands of visitors from around the world to celebrate everything cowboy—including a ranch rodeo competition, chuckwagon cook-off, cowboy poetry and music.

But if you think standard dress in Abilene is jeans and boots, guess again. The city's cultural offerings include ballet, opera, classical chorus, museums and galleries, a zoo, live theater and an orchestra. World-renowned musicians and artists find enthusiastic audiences whose passion for the arts is surpassed only by their love of their Western heritage.

Abilene ... A Whole Lotta Texas Going On.

For more information, contact the Abilene Convention and Visitors Bureau at 1-800-727-7740 or www.abilene.com/visitors

Tom Perini's
Ranch-Roasted Ribeye

Serves 8

Using a 12-pound boneless prime rib, trim excess fat, and cover with Ribeye Rub (below). Place meat on grill, and roast 3 hours at 325 degrees F, or until internal temperature reaches 125 degrees F. Turn meat every hour. Remove from heat, and let rest for at least 40 minutes before serving.

Ribeye Rub:

1	cup coarsely ground salt
2	cups coarsely ground black pepper
$1/3$	cup flour or corn starch
$1/3$	cup garlic powder
$1/3$	cup dried oregano

Ribeye Rub

64

Tom Perini's Cowboy Potatoes

Serves 8-10

4-5	pounds potatoes, cut into wedges
1	stick butter, melted
1	medium white onion, sliced
1-2	cloves garlic, finely minced
1	teaspoon garlic salt
1	teaspoon ground black pepper
$1/2$	teaspoon ground dried oregano

Preheat oven to 350 degrees F. Coat the potatoes in butter, toss with onion and garlic and sprinkle generously with salt, pepper and oregano. Place in a baking dish, cover with aluminum foil and bake for 1 hour, stirring occasionally. After 1 hour, remove the foil, and continue cooking for another 30 minutes to achieve a nice color.

Tom Perini's Buttermilk Biscuits

Makes 24 biscuits

2	cups flour
2	teaspoons baking powder
$1/2$	teaspoon baking soda
$3/4$	teaspoon salt
3	tablespoons vegetable shortening
1	cup buttermilk

Combine the dry ingredients. Add the shortening, and mix well with the back of a mixing spoon. Add the buttermilk, and mix thoroughly. Roll out dough on a floured board to a $1/2$-inch thickness. Cut into rounds, and place on an ungreased baking sheet. Bake at 450 degrees F for approximately 10 minutes, or until browned.

Boston Cream Candy

3 cups sugar
1 cup condensed milk (unsweetened)
$3/4$ cup white karo
1 teaspoon vanilla
Pecans

Mix well. Cook, stirring constantly to keep from burning until 226 degrees F. Remove from heat. Add vanilla and pecans. Beat until creamy. Pour into greased pan.

Prude Ranch Caramel Squares

Prepared by Grandmother Prude for guests beginning in 1922

1	cup butter
2	cups brown sugar
2	cups flour
2	eggs
	Pinch of salt
$1/2$	cup pecans, if desired
1	teaspoon vanilla

Cream butter and 1 cup sugar. Add vanilla, one egg, flour and salt. Press into buttered pan, spread thin. Beat other egg, and smear on top of batter. Sprinkle remaining cup of sugar over egg; add pecans on top of sugar. Bake in 350 degrees F-oven for 20 minutes. Do not overbake. Cut in squares while hot.

Potato Casserole

A favorite dish served at Chuck Wagon Cookouts at Prude Ranch – Betty Prude
Serves 8-10

2	large packages hash brown frozen potatoes
1	large onion or two packages frozen chopped onions (fresh onion should be chopped fine and sautéed in 1 cup margarine)
4	cups sour cream
1	large can (2 quarts of soup concentrate or 4 small cans) of either Cream of Chicken or Cream of Mushroom Soup
4	cups grated cheddar cheese (I usually use more cheese)
	Salt, pepper and cayenne (just a tiny bit of cayenne) sprinkled all over top of ingredients

Mix all ingredients well. Spray Pam in baking dish, and sprinkle the following ingredients on top of casserole mixture:
4 cups crushed corn flakes
2 sticks melted margarine

Bake at least 1 $1/2$ hours in 350 degrees F-oven. Don't rush baking as topping will get too brown. This mixture can be done the day before and left in refrigerator, or even frozen until time of baking.

Big Bend Country

The rugged peaks of a rugged land

Big Bend Country

The Big Bend region stretches across Texas toward the sky with a scattered range of wind-chiseled mountains that reach more than a mile high. There is a far distance between cities and towns, traces of civilization, and the landscape, at times, possesses a tortured moonscape whose beauty has been molded by lava-faced peaks that bespeak of another time on earth, whose canyons are stained gold and purple by long shadows crawling across the Chihuahuan Desert.

The Franklin Mountains, the southernmost tip of the Rockies, is a great wall that hides away El Paso, the pass to the north. Influenced by the traditions and flavor of Mexico, just a stone's throw away across the Rio Grande, the city has its own distinctive culture and lifestyle. Much of El Paso's storied past can be found within the adobe walls of the Fort Bliss replica. The El Paso Museum of Art contains the multimillion dollar Kress Collection, including a Stuart Gilbert Portrait of George Washington. The Bullfight Museum pays tribute to the daring exploits of the Mexican matador. The El Paso Museum of History explores the life and times of Native Americans, conquistadors, vaqueros, cowboys and the U.S. Cavalry. The Galleria Colonial Museum features 18th and 19th century Mexican Colonial art, and Placita Santa Fe houses a Southwestern collection of arts, crafts, antiques and Indian artifacts. Overlooking the lower valley of El Paso—at Ysleta, Socorro and San Elizario—are Spanish missions that date back to the 17th and 18th centuries.

Farther east are the Hueco Tanks, a state park, a great outcropping of rocks in the Hueco Mountains, where nature has carved waterholes into stone. For centuries, they have held water for desert travelers. Names of the gold-hungry forty-niners heading toward California can be seen scratched on the walls of a cave, and pictographs, some dating back two thousand years, recall the cultures of Pueblos, Apaches and Navahos. They are merely road signs in a lonely land that had no road.

Midland relives the dream of coaxing riches from deep within the Permian Basin at its Petroleum Museum, a place to explore five hundred million years of geological history. Boomtown recreates a slice of life from the 1920s with a barbershop, general store, oil field supply store and, of course, a saloon and jail. Theatre Midland offers Broadway style musicals. The Museum of the Southwest chronicles art from the Old Masters to contemporary works. The Confederate Air Force flies the Texas skies overhead with the world's largest, finest and most complete collection of flying World War II aircraft.

67

Big Bend Country

Odessa is a city of surprises. The noted Globe of the Southwest is a recreation of William Shakespeare's original Globe Theatre. Within the Presidential Museum is a storehouse of information on the nation's highest office and the men who called the White House home. Oil lay beneath the sands of Odessa, but the desert terrain around the city was bombarded more than 20,000 years ago by a massive shower of meteorites that collided with the earth. A nature trail winds through the Meteor Crater, whose explosion pit sprawls 500 feet in diameter.

Big Bend is a national park that spreads for 789,000 acres across the wild country south of Marathon, Marfa and Alpine. Some have called it the last frontier, although a rustic lodge and stone cottages now occupy the Chisos Basin. You can discover the Texas Outback by automobile along a paved, winding road that travels from the mouth of Santa Elena Canyon to the sandy slopes of Boquillas Canyon. Another way is to follow hiking trails down to the Window, up along the vistas of Lost Mine Peak or to the South Rim. Stand atop a lonely cliff and, as an old cowboy said, see clear into day after tomorrow. On the western edge of the Big Bend, civilization has crept into Lajitas. A hotel, condominium and golf course development now rests in the solitude and beauty of the landscape, although the walls of the old trading post are scarred by bullets put there by Pancho Villa.

Strange mountains climb boldly above Fort Davis like great gothic towers, overlooking the parade ground of a lonely outpost that stood guard in the hostile country. Fort Davis is a National Historic Site with a museum that houses relics and mementos of the post's thirty-seven years of service against the last stand of the Apache and Comanche nations. Down the road, jammed high into the rocky crest of Mount Locke at 6,800 feet, is the famed McDonald Observatory, probing the stars and beyond with a 107-inch telescope.

The forested peaks of Guadalupe Mountains National Park, northeast of El Paso, have been described as the most rugged country found on the North American continent. The sheer 1,000-foot cliff of El Capitan is the country's most significant Permian fossil reef. Guadalupe Peak is the tallest point in Texas, a magnificent land called home by elk and deer and bobcat. When former Secretary of Interior Stuart Udall hiked the trails cutting precariously along the slopes of the strong, defiant citadel, he said, "The Guadalupes contain the most diversified and beautiful scenery in Texas, some of the most beautiful landscape in the Southwest."

West Texas cattle country

68

Healthy Beef Stew with Vegetables

Indian Cliffs Ranch, Home of the World Famous Cattleman's Steakhouse, El Paso

2   pounds stewing beef
1   large onion, diced
8   beef bouillon cubes
10 cloves garlic, diced
1   bunch cilantro, chopped
1   bunch parsley, chopped
2   pounds frozen vegetables, preferably broccoli, carrots, cauliflower

Cut stewing beef into 1-inch cubes; trim of any fat. Place in large enough pot with 10 cups of water. Add diced onions, cilantro, parsley, garlic and bouillon cubes. Simmer for about 3 hours, or until beef is tender to the fork. (You can use dried cilantro or parsley instead of fresh: use 3 heaping tablespoons of each.)

Add frozen vegetables, and simmer until done, approximately 1 hour. Add water, if necessary, to keep vegetables covered. Stir occasionally.

Season to taste with pepper. Be careful with salt, since the bouillon cubes contain a lot of salt. For some zest, add a splash of hot sauce or 2 to 3 tablespoons of salsa. Stir well.

This recipe is very forgiving and lends itself well to other healthy herbs, like dill weed, chopped chives, etc. A small stalk of celery, diced and added at the beginning, also adds a nice flavor.

Serve as a stew over rice or mashed potatoes, or by itself. Promptly refrigerate any leftovers. It will keep well in the refrigerator for up to 2 weeks and gets better with re-heating.

If this is not the healthiest and best stew you have ever tasted, bring your recipe by the steakhouse, and we will give you a free dessert.

70

Peppers ready for the El Paso chile harvest

El Paso
Heritage of the West

El Paso is a blend of Mexican, Spanish and Native American heritage that combines with a unique and passionate history. Those who visit, whether for business or leisure, are eager to explore and learn of its historical significance, its spectacular landscapes, Spanish architecture and delicious food.

El Paso's sister city, Ciudad Juarez, sits directly across the border in Mexico. The international twin communities are situated in the Chihuahuan Desert and wrap around the base of the rugged Franklin Mountains, the foothills of the majestic Rockies. This unique area enjoys more than 300 days of sunshine each year.

To understand the culture of the area, begin at the Chamizal National Monument. The memorial is the site of a 120-foot-long mural that depicts the blending of both American and Mexican cultures. The site hosts the Onate Historical Festival (The First Thanksgiving), celebrated in 1598 by Spanish Conquistadors on the banks of the Rio Grande. The area was built around the Mission of Our Lady of Guadalupe in 1668 in Juarez. While presently north of the river, the next three churches on the Mission Trail were in Old Mexico before the Rio Grande changed course. The Ysleta Mission is the oldest in Texas, founded in 1682 by Spaniards and Tigua Indians from Ysleta. The area around the mission is home to Speaking Rock Casino and the Tigua Cultural Center. Socorro Mission is the best surviving example of Spanish Colonial/Mexican architecture, and San Elizario Presidio Chapel was built in 1789 to serve as a military fort against the Apache and Comanche.

No visit to El Paso is complete without checking out the most talked-about show in town – Viva! El Paso. McKelligon Canyon provides the backdrop for Viva! – a summer outdoor drama that conveys the history of El Paso, starting from the late 1500's. This musical production features a magnificent display of entertainment, colorful costumes and legendary Viva! Characters.

Feel the exhilaration of being in such a place that has fascinated and excited the human spirit for thousands of years. Your visit allows you to become a part of the rich fabric. We hope to see you soon in El Paso del Norte – The Pass of the North.

Culture across the border

Consuelo's Chicken Salpicon

Forti's Mexican Elder Restaurant, El Paso • Serves 8 to 10

3	chicken breasts, boiled
6	fresh jalapenos, chopped
2	fresh tomatoes, chopped
$1/2$	onion, chopped
$1/4$	cup fresh cilantro, chopped
$1/4$	cup olive oil
$1/4$	cup white vinegar
1	teaspoon salt
1	teaspoon black pepper
2	avocados, cut into small squares

Slice chicken into thin strips, and mix with all of the above ingredients. Add avocado last. Serve on a bed of lettuce.

Mariano's Margarita Pie

Dessert Tacos

Makes 24 servings.

2 cups semi-sweet chocolate chips
1 ounce paraffin
1 box mini taco shells

In a double boiler, melt chocolate chips and paraffin. Meanwhile, place taco shells on baking sheet, and heat at 350 degrees F for 5-7 minutes. Dip each shell in the melted chocolate mixture, coating all sides. Let excess chocolate drip off. Place open end down on a baking sheet lined with wax paper. Let stand until chocolate hardens. Fill each taco with your favorite fruits, ice cream or pudding.

Mariano's Margarita Pie

Serves 6-8.

Crust:

18 graham crackers
$1/2$ pound butter
$1/3$ cup sugar

Filling:

1 package clear gelatin
10 ounces water
4 ounces margarita mix
$1/4$ cup tequila
2 tablespoons sugar
1 (12-ounce) container
   whipped topping
   Zest of two limes

Put graham crackers in blender or food processor, and chop to a very fine consistency. Melt butter and mix into graham crackers. Add sugar, stir well and then press into pie pan. Place crust in freezer for 2 hours to set. Dissolve gelatin in $1/4$ cup warm water. Place in a blender along with remaining water, margarita mix, tequila, sugar and whipped topping. Blend thoroughly. Pour into chilled graham cracker crust. Garnish with a layer of whipped topping. Sprinkle with lime rind shavings.

Puntas de Filete with Chipotle Mushrooms and Jalapeno Au Jus

Cafe Central, El Paso • All amounts are approximate • Serves 6

Puntas:

6 ounces beef tenderloin (all silver skin, fat and membrane trimmed off) thinly sliced into thin medallions

Chipolte Mushrooms:

3 ounces thinly sliced button mushrooms (not canned)
1 chipolte pepper (canned in adobo sauce) depending on how hot you want it
   Chopped cilantro to taste
   Small amount of chopped garlic
$1/4$ of a small red onion, finely chopped
$1/4$ of red onion, sliced into strips
1 cube of beef boullion in small amount of water
   Salt and pepper

Jalapeno Au Jus:

   Equal part Worcestershire sauce and soy sauce
   Sliced red onion
   Roasted jalapeno peppers (add as many as you think you can eat)
2 bay leaves

Combine soy, Worcestershire, roasted jalapeno, red onion and bay leaves. Set aside.

In a small sauté pan, heat a small amount of vegetable or olive oil. When oil is hot, add chopped onion and garlic; when onion starts to turn translucent, add mushrooms, sauté until mushrooms are limp; add chopped chipolte and some of the adobo juice from the can. Add sliced onion and beef bullion, using caution; bullion is salty. Add as much liquid as is desirable. Add cilantro, take off heat and start meat.

In a medium sauté pan, heat a small amount of olive or vegetable oil, salt and pepper the tenderloin and lay in pan, cook until the meat just has color turn and cook until desired doneness.

Lay meat on plate, and scoop a small amount of mushrooms and their juice onto meat; drizzle jalapeno au jus onto meat and mushrooms. (Jalapenos also are great for munching on.)

72

Midland

Gateway To Big Bend

Home of President George W. Bush, Midland welcomes visitors with its famous, friendly West Texas attitude and exceptional climate. Sunny days, cool evenings and low humidity create pleasant conditions for endless activities.

Outstanding museums span a broad range of interests. Visitors can view vintage aircraft and authentic WWII memorabilia at the Confederate Air Force's American Airpower Heritage Museum, walk "under" an ancient sea at the unique Petroleum Museum or enjoy a comprehensive collection of American Southwestern art and archaeology at the Museum of the Southwest.

A new terminal at Midland International Airport, as well as Interstate 20 and other state highways, make travel in and out of the Big Bend region an uncomplicated, enjoyable experience. Visitors can enjoy great shopping at 600 retailers, dining at 100 restaurants, excellent theaters, driving tours and the end of a memorable day by relaxing in one of the many elegant, yet economical hotels.

Call 1-800-624-6435 or visit www.midlandtx.com

Midland Texas – In the Middle of Somewhere

George W. Bush Brisket

This recipe, donated by Danny's Deli in Midland, makes a great brisket sandwich, and it is a favorite of President George W. Bush.

8-10 pounds brisket
Your favorite marinade
Salt and pepper
5 cups water

Place brisket fat side up in a deep roasting pan. Pierce with knife several times. Pour marinade over brisket, and add water to cover $^3/_4$ of meat. Salt and pepper to taste. Cover with foil, and set in refrigerator overnight.

Preheat oven to 300 degrees F. Cook about 40 minutes per pound. Remove from pan, drain and save marinade.

NOTE: *It is easier to slice when cold. Refrigerate. Slice and pour marinade over meat. Cover and reheat for 1 hour. Ready to serve.*

Laura Bush's Cowboy Cookies

Provided by Jenna Welch, Midland, Mother of Laura Bush
Makes 3 dozen cookies

3 cups flour
1 tablespoon baking powder
1 tablespoon baking soda
1 tablespoon cinnamon
1 teaspoon salt
3 sticks butter at room temperature
1 cup white sugar
1 $^1/_2$ cups packed light brown sugar
3 eggs
1 tablespoon vanilla
3 cups semisweet chocolate chips
3 cups old-fashioned rolled oats
2 cups sweetened flake coconut
2 cups chopped pecans

Preheat oven to 350 degrees F. Mix flour, baking powder, baking soda, cinnamon and salt in bowl.

George W. Bush with wife Laura and Laura's Mother, Jenna Welch

Photo courtesy of the Petroleum Museum

In 8-quart bowl, beat butter on medium speed till smooth and creamy, about 1 minute. Gradually beat in sugars, and continue beating to combine, about 2 minutes. Add eggs, 1 at a time, beating after each. Beat in vanilla. Stir in flour mixture until just combined. Add chocolate chips, oats, coconut and pecans.

For each cookie, drop $^1/_4$ cup of dough onto an ungreased cookie sheet, spacing them 3-inches apart. Bake for 17-20 minutes, or until edges are lightly browned. Remove to rack and let cool.

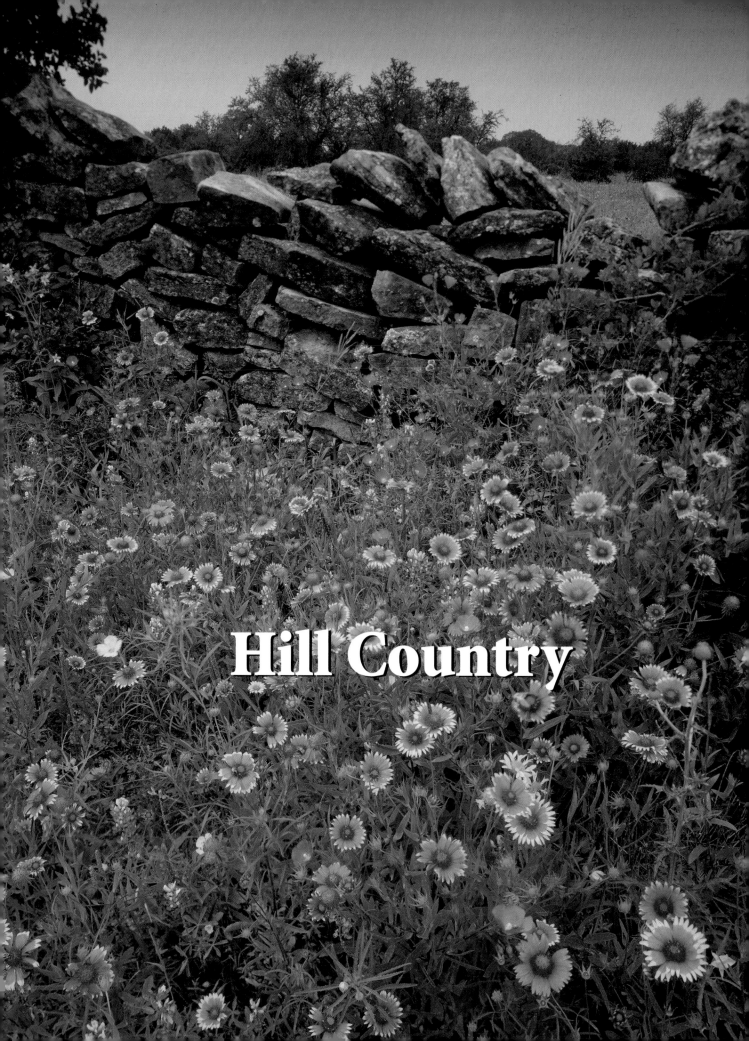

Hill Country

The rugged hills, ablaze in springtime with the vibrant colors of bluebonnets and Indian paintbrush, rise up with broad, strong shoulders above the Texas backbone, a chunk of old-fashioned Western legacy as solid as the pink granite beneath its soil. Severe canyons slice through juniper flats. Winding rivers slip beneath the aching limbs of knock-kneed cypress. Whitetail deer abound, and the glorious chain of Highland Lakes—Travis, Buchanan, LBJ, Inks, Marble Falls, Austin and Canyon—quench the valleys of a sun-spackled land.

The Germans draped their gingerbread architecture from the balconies of Fredericksburg and New Braunfels. The French left a trace of the Alsace at Castroville. Forts, which once protected the frontier, lie scattered like weathered tombstones among the hills. As President Lyndon B. Johnson wrote of the hills, "It was once barren land. The angular hills were covered with scrub cedar and few live oak ... But men came and worked and endured and built."

Culture has long been a revered cornerstone of Austin. The Elisabet Ney Museum focuses on the life and work of a noted German sculptress. Laguna Gloria is a museum for twentieth century art, and the Harry Ransom Center showcases fine works of art, Greek and roman sculpture, Western paintings and one of only five Gutenberg Bibles in the United States, printed in 1455.

But the capital city honors its past with distinctive monuments as well. The French Legation remains as the oldest home in Austin. Museums are dedicated to both the Daughters of the Republic of Texas and Daughters of the Confederacy. The George Washington Carver Museum and Madison Cabin underscore the African American heritage of Texas. The Jourdan-Bachman Pioneer Farm, once blanketed by 2,000 acres of cotton, is a living history museum. Memories, artifacts and documents within the Lyndon B. Johnson Presidential Library trace Johnson's rise to political power, becoming the most influential Senate Majority Leader in the nation's history, running for the vice presidency and finally ascending to the highest office in the land when the torch was passed to him aboard Air Force One amidst one of the country's darkest days.

Johnson was a son of the Hill Country, and his legacy is forever rooted along the Pedernales River that runs beside his homeland. In and around Johnson City are his restored boyhood home, a national historic site, his birthplace and his ranch, known as the Texas White House.

Near Fredericksburg, Enchanted Rock is a great granite blister that early Native Americans believed was holy and sacred. Fredericksburg blends the Old World charm of Bavaria with the Old West touch of Texas by surrounding a dude ranch or two with bed and breakfast houses, some historic, some rustic and some Victorian. New Braunfels is proud of its German heritage as well, famed for its annual Wurstfest where thousands gather dressed in dirndls and lederhosen or faded jeans and cowboy boots to pay homage to sausage. But the curious beauty of the Texas Hill Country lies beneath the crust of the earth, down within Natural Bridge Caverns, a fantasy world formed from limestone more than 140 million years ago.

San Marcos crowns the hills, surrounding Aquarena Springs that once served as an oasis for Spanish explorers wandering through the high country. Glass-bottom boats ferry guests across Spring Lake to observe the fish and plant life beneath its surface, and costumed mermaids perform in the underwater shows of Submarine Theatre. Not far away, Wonder Cave, lying in the heart of seven-acre Juniper Forest Wildlife Park, was created by the anger and chaos of a long-ago earthquake.

Bandera has become the Cowboy Capital of Texas with its guest ranches that offer a touch of luxury amidst the harsh realities of cattle country. The cowboy image is branded deeply in the hills around Kerrville. Vivid portraits of the Old West hang on the walls of the Cowboy Artists of America Museum. The Y.O. Ranch in nearby Mountain Home is grazed by such exotic game as zebras, giraffes, antelopes and even the fringe-eared oryx.

And the harsh landscape around Del Rio and Mexico is flooded by the waters of Lake Amistad, which calls itself the Crown Jewel of Texas Lakes. The mammoth Amistad Dam impounds 67,000 surface acres of water, making it the third largest international manmade lake in the world. Its shoreline has become a haven for fishermen, as well as explorers who can ease their boats into Seminole Canyon to view some of the most striking Indian pictographs ever drawn by the hand of prehistoric man.

Hill country wildflowers

Barbecue Fish Bake

Serves 6.

6	fish fillets
	Oil
1	teaspoon salt
2	tablespoons sweet vermouth
1	bottle barbecue sauce
$1/2$	cup minced celery, sautéed
$1/4$	cup slivered almonds
$1/4$	cup minced green onions for garnish

Place fish fillets in oiled baking dish, and sprinkle with salt. In a bowl, mix wine, barbecue sauce, celery and almonds. Pour mixture over fish. Bake at 350 degrees F for about 20 minutes, or until fish flakes. Garnish with onions.

Lemon Garlic Turkey Tenders

Serves 6.

1	tablespoon grated lemon peel
$1/2$	cup lemon juice
2	cloves garlic, diced fine
$1/4$	cup cooking oil
1	tablespoon soy sauce
6	(8-ounce) tenderloins
$1/2$	cup flour
2	teaspoons paprika
2	sheets heavy duty aluminum foil 24 inches long

Mix peel, juice, garlic, oil and soy sauce, marinade turkey tenders 3 hours or longer (overnight is ideal). Save marinade; coat turkey tenders with flour and paprika. Place 3 turkey tenders on each piece of foil, brush with marinade. Fold foil seal tightly. Bake 30 minutes at 350 degrees F. Open foil, turn turkey tenders; brush again with marinade. Continue cooking 30 minutes longer at 300 degrees.

Rice Cornbread Bake

Serves 8-10.

1	cup yellow or white cornmeal
$1/2$	teaspoon salt
$1/2$	teaspoon baking soda
2	cups cooked rice, white or brown
1	cup low fat milk
1	(8 3/4-ounce) can cream-style corn
2	eggs, beaten
$1/2$	cup chopped jalapeno pepper
1	tablespoon vegetable oil
$3/4$	cup shredded Monterey Jack cheese

Combine cornmeal, salt and soda in bowl, stirring well. Add remaining ingredients except cheese. Pour into 12 x 8 x 2-inch baking pan that has been coated with cooking spray. Bake at 350 degrees F for 45 minutes or until lightly browned. Sprinkle cheese on top, and return to oven until cheese melts.

Curried Rice Stuffing

Makes 4-5 servings or stuffings for 1 roasted chicken.

1 $1/2$	cups precooked rice
1 $1/2$	cups Dr Pepper
$1/2$	teaspoon curry powder
$1/2$	cup chopped pecans or almonds
2	tablespoons butter

Cook rice according to package directions, except substitute Dr Pepper for the water. Add curry powder to the Dr Pepper before cooking. Toast nuts in butter, and add to cooked rice, mixing lightly. Use as a stuffing for game or fowl, or separately with game or fowl.

Pecan Croquettes

Makes 16 croquettes.

1	tablespoon minced onion
1	tablespoon chopped green pepper
2	tablespoons shortening
3	cups unseasoned mashed potatoes
2	cups pecan pieces
1	tablespoon chopped parsley
1	egg, beaten
1	teaspoon salt
$1/8$	teaspoon pepper
$1/2$	teaspoon Worcestershire sauce
1	egg
1	tablespoon water
	Fine dry breadcrumbs

Sauté onion, green pepper and shortening over medium heat for 5 minutes. Add mashed potatoes, pecans, parsley, 1 beaten egg, salt, pepper and Worcestershire sauce to vegetables, and shape into croquettes. Beat together 1 egg and water. Roll croquettes in fine breadcrumbs. Dip in egg mixture, then roll in crumbs again. Let stand 10 minutes to form slight crust. Fry in deep hot fat (375 degrees-400 degrees F) until golden brown. Serve hot with mushroom or cheese sauce, if desired.

Austin

Place of A Lifetime

In naming Austin among its "50 Places of a Lifetime," National Geographic Traveler declares that "Only in Austin could Willie Nelson have brought hippies and rednecks together under one tin roof at the Armadillo World Headquarters." And in doing so, he unwittingly spawned the origins of a progressive music scene that, more than a half-century later, brands Austin as the "Live Music Capital of the World."

While known for being many things to many people, Austin relies on the music for its soul. On any given evening, live music plays at more than 100 venues.

There's much more to the state capital of Texas. Home to the University of Texas. Entryway to the high-tech Silicon Hills. Vast greenbelts and sweeping landscapes. Long revered as the playground of Texas, Austin sits at the center of the Lone Star State and stands as gateway to the rolling Texas Hill Country.

Blessed with 300 days of sunshine a year, Austin lives for the outdoors. An incredible mix of nature trails, parks and wilderness preserves create an environmental paradise. Town Lake streams through the heart of the city and blesses it with a distinct natural beauty.

Along with its eclectic character, Austin shows off a very sophisticated side. One of only a handful of cities to stage professional symphony, opera, ballet and theater companies, the city plays host to nationally acclaimed film festivals and countless dining options.

Among the most popular attractions are the Texas State Capitol, Lyndon B. Johnson Presidential Library and the Bob Bullock Texas State History Museum, where the myth and fact of the legendary state come together under one roof.

Texas State Capital

Pecan Crusted Beef Tenderloin With Jalapeno Mashed Potatoes and Sweet Corn Sauce

Executive Chef David J. Bull, the Driskill Grill, Austin
Serves 4

Beef Tenderloin

4   beef tenderloins
    salt to taste
    pepper to taste
3   ounces canola oil

Preheat oven to 400 degrees F. Season tenderloin on all sides with salt and pepper, and sear each filet over high heat in a large sauté pan in the canola oil. Sear each filet until all sides are golden brown. Place the filets into a preheated 400 degrees F-oven, and cook until desired doneness. Remove from oven, and spread with the pecan crust on one side. Place back into the preheated oven for 2-3 minutes, or until the pecan crust is golden brown. Reserve hot until ready to serve.

continued on next page

77

Pecan Crust

6	ounces pecan pieces, toasted and ground
2	ounces Dijon mustard
2	ounces honey
	Salt to taste

In a mixing bowl, combine all ingredients, and season with salt. Reserve for the beef tenderloin.

Jalapeno Mashed Potatoes

3	Idaho potatoes, peeled and cut into even pieces
	Water as needed
	Salt to taste
1	cup heavy whipping cream
3	ounces whole salted butter
5	jalapenos, roasted, skin and seeds removed, diced

In a large sauce pot, cover the potatoes with water, season with salt and bring to a boil. Cook over medium heat until the potatoes are fork tender. Combine the heavy cream and the butter, and bring mixture to a boil in a small sauce pot over medium heat. Strain the potatoes. In a mixing bowl, add potatoes and half the cream butter mixture, and whip until blended. Add the remaining cream butter mixture as needed to obtain proper consistency of mashed potatoes. Add the roasted and diced jalapenos, and season with salt to taste. Reserve hot until ready to serve.

Sweet Corn Sauce

1	ounce canola oil
1	shallot, chopped
1	teaspoon cumin, ground
3	ears of corn, shucked—kernels removed
1	cup chicken stock
	Lime juice to taste
	Salt to taste
	Maple syrup to taste

In a small sauce pot over medium heat, add the canola oil. Add the shallot, and sauté for 1 minute. Add the ground cumin, and toast for 1 minute. Add the shucked kernels of corn, and cook for 1 minute. Add the chicken stock, bring to a boil and cook for 5 minutes. Place mixture into a blender, and puree until smooth. Strain through a fine mesh sieve, and season with lime juice, salt and maple syrup to taste. Reserve hot until ready to serve.

To Serve:

On four large, warm dinner plates, spoon jalapeno mashed potatoes into the center of each plate. Place one filet in the center of the mashed potatoes. Ladle sweet corn sauce around the plate.

Beef Kabobs Over Lemon Rice

Makes 2 servings.

$1/2$	pound beef boneless sirloin steak, cut into 1-inch cubes
1	small zucchini, cut in chunks
1	small yellow squash, cut in squares
1	small onion, cut in chunks
$1/4$	cup gourmet garnishes

Oriental dressing

1	cup hot cooked rice
2	teaspoons fresh lemon juice
1	tablespoon parsley, snipped
$1/4$	teaspoon seasoning salt

Combine beef and vegetables in plastic bag with zippered closing. Add salad dressing, and marinate 4-6 hours in refrigerator. Alternate beef and vegetables on 4 skewers. Grill or boil with remaining marinade 5-7 minutes, or to desired doneness. To prepare Lemon Rice, combine rice, and add remaining ingredients. Serve kabobs over Lemon Rice.

Summer Fruit Salad with Raspberry Dressing

Serves 4-6.

1	cup seedless grapes
1	apple, cored and cubed
1	cup cantaloupe, cubed
1	cup honeydew melon, cubed
1	cup orange wedges, peeled
1	cup watermelon, seeded and cubed
1	cup fresh strawberries, stemmed and sliced
1	cup walnuts or pecans, chopped
	Mint leaves to garnish

Dressing:

$1/2$	cup brown sugar
$1/4$	cup raspberry vinaigrette (basil-lime vinaigrette can be substituted)
1	cup fruit yogurt

In a bowl, add brown sugar to the raspberry dressing; whisk until sugar is dissolved. While whisking, add the yogurt to a smooth consistency. Pour over the fruits; toss lightly. Serve in wine cup as a dessert or light summer salad. Decorate with mint leaves.

The celebration of Wurstfest

New Braunfels Smokehouse Bread Pudding

Serves 6-8

PUDDING

4	eggs
1	cup sugar
4	cups milk
2	teaspoons vanilla
1 $^1/_2$	loaves bread, cubed
3	ounces raisins
$^1/_2$ cup	brown sugar

Beat eggs and sugar in a bowl. Add vanilla and milk, and beat. Add bread and raisins. Mix well. Put in two 9x9x2-inch loaf pans. Sprinkle each pan with 1/4 cup brown sugar. Bake at 350 degrees F for 30 minutes, or until pudding has risen to top of pan. Serve warm, topped with butter sauce.

BUTTER SAUCE

$^3/_4$	cup sugar
3	beaten egg yolks
3	tablespoons melted butter
2	tablespoons cornstarch (dissolved in $^1/_4$ cup water)
1 $^1/_2$	cups boiling water
2	teaspoons vanilla
$^1/_8$	teaspoon salt

In double boiler, cream sugar, eggs and butter. Add starch mixture. Then add boiling water slowly. Cook over hot water until thickened, stirring constantly. Add vanilla and salt.

New Braunfels

Old World Charm

Nestled in the gateway of the Texas Hill Country, New Braunfels opens wide and embraces Old World charm and hometown hospitality. Founded in 1845, this German town is steeped in heritage featured in six museums and over 40 festivals. The settlers landed in this garden spot because of the beautiful rivers. The Guadalupe and Comal Rivers feature water recreation year-round: tubing, rafting, fly fishing and good old "swimmin' holes." Quaint downtown New Braunfels and Historic Gruene are a shopper's dream, with one of a kind treasures around every corner. Cuisine is varied and bountiful. German, Mexican, Italian, Family and Southern dining are a treat! Who else has a 10-day festival saluting sausage!

79

Piney Woods

Dogwoods in the Big Thicket

Piney Woods

The Piney Woods of Texas shade Victorian communities that are old-fashioned, proud of their past and deeply Southern. Roadways cut through thick tunnels of green, winding past national forests, cotton fields and on across a goodly land where great rivers of oil await beneath the earth.

In the 1930s, the towering pines were stained with the drippings of oil around Kilgore, Longview, Tyler, Gladewater, Henderson and Overton. In the words of the aging wildcatter who drilled the discovery well, he had tapped into "a treasure trove that all the kings of the earth might covet." It became the nation's largest producing field of petroleum.

The Piney Woods are bordered on the north by the Red River and on the east by the Sabine River. Steamboats once churned down Cypress Bayou, headed toward Jefferson back when it was the second largest port city in Texas. It has been awarded more historical medallions than any other community in the state, with forty-six of them hanging on its homes, churches and buildings. Winnsboro basks in the gold-lacquered leaves of its Autumn Trails. Gilmer's Yamboree pays homage to the sweet potato.

Iron ore was gouged from the red earth around Daingerfield. Mount Pleasant rose up alongside a mysterious, hand-hewn earthen temple built by some pre-historic race, and the Caddoes called it "Pleasant Mound." Texarkana is a city with two homes, its State Line Avenue straddling the border of Texas and Arkansas. The Texarkana Historical Museum traces the good life and the hard life before and after the coming of the railroad.

The Texas State Railroad links Palestine with Rusk, the woodlands blanketed by dogwoods during spring. Alto has never been able to decipher the riddle of the ceremonial mounds along the Neches River. A salt dome far beneath the soil of Grand Saline could supply the world's need for salt during the next 20,000 years. Karnack is the gateway to Caddo Lake, formed, a Native American elder said, when the earth had fever, then chills, and quaked at night. And Carthage remembers the voices of Jim Reeves and Tex Ritter, whose songs were anthems for the working man, as honest as the ground beneath a farmer's feet.

Athens has a culinary link to legendary food in Texas. The city gained a certain amount of notoriety when Uncle Fletch Davis invented the first genuine, honest-to-goodness hamburger. And now Athens has gained prominence as the "Black-Eyed Pea Capital of the World," with thousands coming to the Black-Eyed Pea jamboree to watch a pea-rade, hear

81

Piney Woods

pea-pickin' and singin', enter pea poppin' and pea shellin' contests and taste dishes from an abundance of prize-winning reci-peas.

The flag of Missouri flew above Marshall during the War Between the States when the Missouri governor fled the conflict storming across his state. For more than a century, its potters have been mining their clay from those pine-clad hills, turning out more than a million pots a year. Marshall reflects the aristocracy of its heritage with more than twenty National Register historic properties, as well a several beautiful old bed and breakfast inns.

Tyler has gained fame as the Rose Capital of the World, and Tyler has the credentials to prove it. The city boasts the nation's largest municipal rose garden, with more than 30,000 plants blooming across fourteen acres. A special Heritage Rose and Sensory Garden contains varieties of nineteenth century garden roses, dating back to 1867. In fact, one-fifth of all commercially grown rose bushes in the world come from two hundred nurseries in Smith County, and most of the ten to twenty million rose plants produced in Texas are grown within a fifty-mile radius of Tyler. In October of each year, the community pays tribute to the industry with its celebrated Rose Festival.

San Augustine became known as the "Cradle of Texas." Nacogdoches remembers the past with its Old Stone Fort, built only a year after the colonies announced their independence from Great Britain. It was a trading post, a refuge, a fortress, a courthouse, and within its walls were published the first two newspapers in Texas. Lufkin is gateway to Lake Sam Rayburn, and its Texas Forestry Museum takes a historic look at its tall timber skyline and the lumberjacks who built the logging industry. Crockett's Mission Tejas was the first Spanish chapel in East Texas, a reconstructed relic of the 1690s.

The Alabama-Coushatta Indian Reservation sprawls across 4,600 acres of verdant timberland that lie in the heart of the Big Thicket between Woodville and Livingston. The land was given them by Sam Houston as a reward for their courage during the Texas War for Independence. In a living Indian village, tribesmen weave baskets from pine needles, make arrows and fashion pottery from clay. The memories of Sam Houston pervade the streets of Huntsville as well. The Sam Houston Memorial Museum crowns fifteen acres of the general's original homestead, and the Steamboat House became his home when he left his office as governor of Texas.

Fog dancing across Caddo Lake

82

Spring Stir-Fry

Serves 6.

1 tablespoon sesame oil
1 tablespoon vegetable oil
1 pound turkey breast slices, cut into thin strips
2 cloves garlic, minced
2 tablespoons soy sauce
1 cup mushrooms, sliced
4 green onions with tops, sliced
2 medium zucchini or yellow squash, sliced
1 package bean sprouts
1 green pepper, cut into strips
1 cup cashew nuts, toasted
2 cups cooked long grain rice

Place sesame oil and vegetable oil in wok or deep skillet over high heat. Add turkey and garlic; stir-fry for about 3 minutes. Add soy sauce, mushrooms, scallions, zucchini or yellow squash, bean sprouts, pepper and cashews. Stir to combine; cover and cook over medium-low heat for 8-10 minutes. Stir occasionally, and test turkey and vegetables for desired doneness. Serve with cooked rice.

Hopping John

Serves 6-8.

1 onion, chopped
1 bell pepper, chopped
1 pound sausage, sliced
2 cups dried blackeyed peas, cooked (measure before cooking)
1 $\frac{1}{2}$ cups cooked rice

Sauté onion, pepper and sausage in large skillet. Combine all ingredients. Serve hot.

Pear Cobbler

Pears were more readily available than apples in this part of East Texas. Huntsville has abundant pear trees around its Woodland Home garden. • Serves 6-8

Pastry:

1 $\frac{1}{2}$ cups sifted all-purpose flour
$\frac{1}{2}$ teaspoon salt
$\frac{1}{4}$ cup shortening
1 egg
3 tablespoons water
4 cups thinly sliced pears (approximately 3 large)
3 tablespoons butter

Filling:

$\frac{1}{2}$ cup sugar
2 tablespoons flour
1 teaspoon nutmeg

Sauce:

1 pear
1 cup water
$\frac{1}{2}$ cup sugar
2 teaspoons cornstarch
$\frac{1}{4}$ teaspoon nutmeg
3 tablespoons butter

Make the pastry by sifting the flour, and salt together in a bowl. Cut in shortening with two knives or a pastry blender until the mixture looks mealy. Beat egg and water together slightly, and stir into the flour combination to form a soft ball of pastry. Start that oven at 350 degrees F. Roll the pastry, which you have chilled for a while, on a floured board into a rectangle about 15 inches by 12 inches in size. Mix sugar, flour and nutmeg together, and sprinkle half the mixture over the pastry. Cover with the peeled, thinly sliced pears. Scatter remaining sugar over the mixture, and dot with butter. Roll pastry as you would a jelly roll, and transfer to a large, shallow baking pan. Bake 50 minutes; but after 30 minutes are up, brush the surface with some of the syrup that leaks out of the cobbler. This gives the top a golden shine.

Last of all, make the sauce while the cobbler bakes. Cut the peeled, cored pear into little cubes. Cook in water for 15 minutes, and in a separate bowl combine sugar, cornstarch and nutmeg. Stir into the cooked pears along with the butter, and continue cooking until the sauce is clear and bubbly. Serve the sauce warm over the cobbler.

Sam Houston Woodland Home, Huntsville

Marshall

A Slice of History

Whether you're looking for a slice of history that's been lovingly restored or life in the fast lane, Marshall is the spot you've been looking for. With its museums, performing arts, potteries and outlet stores, Victorian homes, World Champion Junior Barrel Races and three college campuses, Marshall is definitely the place to be. Nestled among the piney woods of East Texas and located between Lake O' the Pines and historic Caddo Lake, Marshall offers something for every member of the family.

Come experience our special events throughout the year – Stagecoach Days in the spring, Fire Ant Festival in the fall and Wonderland of Lights from Thanksgiving to New Year's. During Wonderland of Lights, view more than ten million tiny white lights and ice skating on the downtown square, tour Victorian homes, then take a carriage ride or a guided bus tour through the several miles of displays. In Marshall, you don't just see the lights; you experience the true spirit of Christmas.

Check us out at www.marshalltxchamber.com, or give us a call at 1-800-953-7868.

The Christmas lights of Marshall

Mrs. Ruby Moyers' Recipe for Tea Cakes

Ruby and Henry Moyers moved to Marshall with sons James and Bill when the latter was a preschooler. Bill Moyers worked as a reporter for the Marshall News Messenger at age 16, graduated with honors from Marshall High School and served in the Kennedy and Johnson administrations before returning to his first love, journalism. He now produces his own documentaries for public television and has been called "the conscience" of the television industry.

His mother, called "Miss Ruby" by Marshallites and her son's colleagues alike, kept these cookies on hand for neighborhood children long after her own were grown and gone.

continued on next page

85

Mrs. Ruby Moyers' Recipe for Tea Cakes

Cream Together:

$1/2$ cup butter-flavored Crisco
4 packages Sweet N' Low
$1/2$ cup sugar
1 egg

Sift Together:

2 cups flour
$1/2$ teaspoon salt
2 teaspoons baking powder
$1/2$ teaspoon soda

Add original mixture, alternating with $1/4$ cup buttermilk and 1 teaspoon vanilla. Roll cookie mixture into a roll, and pinch off dough in size cookie desired; place on baking sheet. Then press down with glass covered with cup towel and dipped in sugar. Bake at 350 degrees F until edges of cookies are brown. Don't try to use a terrycloth towel for this recipe; the fabric should be a muslin-type.

Blackeyes and Rice Salad

Serves 4.

$1/2$ cup mayonnaise
2 tablespoons lemon juice
1 teaspoon Italian seasoning
$1/2$ teaspoon dillweed
   Salt and pepper, to taste
1 (16-ounce) can sliced carrots, drained
1 (15-ounce) can fresh shelled blackeyed peas, drained
2 cups cooked long grain rice
1 stalk celery, sliced
1 green onion, chopped

Combine mayonnaise, lemon juice, Italian seasoning, dillweed, salt and pepper. Stir to blend. Place carrots, blackeyed peas, rice celery and onion in serving dish. Spoon dressing over, and stir gently to coat. Cover and refrigerate until chilled.

Candied Sweet Potatoes

Serves 6.

2 pounds sweet potatoes (about 4 medium potatoes)
1 cup Dr Pepper
$3/4$ cup granulated sugar
$1/4$ cup butter
$1/2$ teaspoon salt

Parboil potatoes 10 minutes. Place in cold water for 5-10 minutes. Remove from water, peel and slice crosswise into casserole. Combine Dr Pepper, sugar, butter and salt. Bring to boil. Boil 10 minutes. Pour over potatoes. Bake at 375 degrees F about 45 minutes. Baste potatoes several times with syrup as potatoes bake.

Beef Tenderloin Fit for a King

Bill Palmer, Marshall • Serves 32-48

4 whole tenderloins (4 pounds each), trimmed and tied
2 cups Worcestershire sauce
$1/2$ cup bourbon (not blended)
4 garlic cloves, minced
3 -inch piece fresh ginger, thinly sliced
$1/4$ cup granulated sugar
1 tablespoon ground pepper
1 cup rock salt (or kosher coarse salt)
2 cups confectioners sugar

In a medium bowl, combine Worcestershire sauce, bourbon, garlic, ginger, sugar and pepper. Put tenders in non-reactive containers. Pour marinade over meat. Marinate 2 hours at room temperature, turning and basting occasionally. Cover and refrigerate over night. Preheat oven to 500 degrees F. On a large baking sheet, combine coarse salt and powdered sugar. Remove and drain tenders. Gently roll the meat in the mixture to coat lightly. Place tenders without touching each other on baking sheets. Set on oven rack on lower shelf. Roast for 12 minutes. Alternate pans and roast for 12 minutes longer. Remove from oven, and cool to room temperature. These can be wrapped and refrigerated up to two days. Let come to room temperature before serving.

Huntsville

From its founding as a trading post in 1836, Huntsville quickly established itself as a prominent Texas town. A thriving downtown historic district with nearly 20 historic markers prompted state officials to name Huntsville a 2001 Main Street City. The Sam Houston Memorial Museum Complex features an impressive collection of original structures such as Houston's Woodland Home and the Steamboat House. Just across from Huntsville State Park is a larger-than-life tribute to Sam Houston, the world's tallest statue of an American hero, along with a visitor center. For a fascinating look at life-and-death-behind prison walls, visit the Texas Prison Museum. Exhibits include confiscated prison-made weapons, prisoners' art and crafts and the electric chair nicknamed "Old Sparky." At the HEARTS Veterans Museum, see thousands of military-related exhibits while local Veterans tell their amazing stories first-hand.

The giant statue of Sam Houston

Margaret Houston's White Cake

Makes One 9-inch Three-Layered Cake

$3/4$	cups butter, softened
2	cups sugar
3	cups all-purpose flour
1	tablespoon baking powder
$1/2$	teaspoon salt
$1/2$	cup milk
$1/2$	cup water
1	teaspoon vanilla extract
1	teaspoon almond extract
6	egg whites

Cream butter and sugar, beating until smooth. Combine flour, baking powder and salt. Combine milk and water. Add flour mixture to creamed mixture, alternately with milk mixture, beginning and ending with flour mixture. Mix well after each addition. Stir in flavoring. Beat egg whites (at room temperature) until soft peaks form, and then fold into the batter. Pour into 3 greased and floured 9-inch round cake pans. Bake at 350 degrees F for 25 minutes, or until a wooden pick inserted into the center comes out clean. Cool in pans 10 minutes before removing the layers to cool completely.

Tyler's Yellow Rose of Texas

Tyler
Legacy of Roses

Visitors who come to Texas expecting to see only oil wells and cactus are amazed by the flourishing beauty of East Texas. What seems even more surprising to the Old West ideal are the famous Tyler Roses. Approximately one-fifth of all commercial rose bushes produced in the United States are grown in Smith County, while over one-half of the nation's rose bushes are packaged and shipped from this area.

This burgeoning industry, which began more than 100 years ago, has established Tyler as the Rose Capital of the Nation. It is only fitting that the City of Roses is home to the nation's largest Municipal Rose Garden. From late April until frost, the Tyler Municipal Rose Garden blooms with more than 30,000 rose bushes and 450 varieties of roses. More than 100,000 people visit the Rose Garden annually.

Rose City Salad

Serves 6-8

6	handfuls mixed salad greens
1	handful fancy baby greens including:
	Orach, violets, ornamental cabbage, mizuna, Tatsoi, amaranth and mache
6-8	large pink ornamental cabbage leaves for garnish
2-3	tablespoons champagne vinegar or white-wine vinegar
	Salt and pepper to taste
1	small clove garlic, finely minced (optional)
4-5	tablespoons extra-virgin olive oil
1	tablespoon finely chopped fresh mint or basil
	Young rose petals and other pink, blue, and white pesticide-free flowers for garnish (choose from strawberry blossoms, violas pansies or violets)

Wash greens well, and dry in a salad spinner. Line a large bowl with the leaves of ornamental cabbage; fill bowl with the greens. In a small bowl, mix the vinegar, salt, pepper and garlic. Whisk in the oil. Add herbs and stir. Just before serving, sprinkle the dressing over the greens. Arrange flowers over the salad, and serve immediately.

Heat N' Sweet Barbecued Chicken

Serves 4-6.

1   jar barbecue sauce
1/2   cup dry sherry or sparkling water
6-8   pieces chicken

Place barbecue sauce in blender, add sherry or water. Blend enough to combine well, and break up tomato pieces. Clean and pat chicken dry. Place chicken in dish, and pour sauce over chicken, coating both sides. Cover and refrigerate about 1 hour. Remove chicken from sauce (reserve sauce), and cook slowly on grill or in the oven until tender. Turn and baste often.

Green Rice

Serves 4.

$1/4$ cup butter
$1/2$ cup chopped onions
1   (15-ounce) can chopped spinach, drained
1   cup cooked rice
$3/4$ (3-ounce) cup grated sharp cheddar cheese
1   (10 $3/4$–ounce) can condensed cream of
      mushroom soup, undiluted
$1/4$ cup milk
$1/8$ teaspoon pepper
2   tablespoons grated
      Parmesan cheese

Preheat oven to 325 degrees F. Melt butter in small skillet over medium-high heat. Add onions and sauté 5 minutes until tender; set aside. Squeeze spinach, onions, rice and cheddar cheese in medium bowl. Add soup, milk and pepper, and stir until well combined. Spoon into 1 $1/2$-quart casserole. Sprinkle with Parmesan cheese. Bake 30 minutes until set.

Cornbread Salad

Serves 6-8.

1   pan cornbread, cooked
1   pint mayonnaise
2   stalks celery, chopped
1   large bell pepper, chopped
1   (2-ounce) can diced pimentos
1   cup chopped green onions and tops
$1/2$ cup pecans, chopped
1   large tomato, diced

Crumble cornbread in bowl. Mix all ingredients, and stir. Place in refrigerator to chill.

Ham with Champagne and Oranges

Serves 3-4.

1   thick ham slice
2   onions
2   oranges
$1/4$ cup brown sugar
1   small lemon
      Texas champagne

Place ham in casserole dish. Score around edge of ham. Chop onions and place on top of ham. Peel oranges and cut in medium-thick slices, and place on top of onions. Sprinkle brown sugar on top of oranges. Slice lemon without peeling, and place slices over brown sugar. Pour $1/4$ to $1/3$ bottle of champagne over all. Bake in 350 degree F-oven for 45 minutes.

Peach Glazed Pork Ribs

Serves 4-6.

$4 – 4 \, 1/2$ pounds pork ribs, cut into serving pieces
$1 – 1 \, 1/2$ cups picante sauce
$1 \, 1/2$ cups peach preserves
$1/4$ cup soy sauce

Place ribs in shallow roasting pan with meaty side up. Bake uncovered in 350 degree F-oven 45 minutes. Heat picante sauce, preserves and soy sauce to boiling, stirring constantly. Brush pork with about $1/2$ cup of the sauce. Bake until tender, 45-60 minutes. Baste ribs several times while baking.

Texas Caviar

Makes 2 cups

1   pound blackeyed peas
2   slices pepper bacon
      Salt, to taste
$1/4$–$1/2$ jar green tomato relish

Cook peas as directed, seasoning with bacon and salt. When peas are cooked, remove from heat, drain and spoon green tomato relish on top.

Raise your glass to Texas. From red and white wines to blush and even champagne, the variety and quality of Texas wines are a testament to the dedication and commitment to excellence of the state's grape growers and wine makers. Texas culinary delights are best when served with a glass of Texas wine. Pour a glass and enjoy the experience!

Texas Wine & Food Pairings

The following chart may give you some guidelines for food and wine pairings.
Key: 1 = Good; 2 = Better; 3 = Best

Foods:	White			Blush	Red		
	Light	Med	Full		Light	Med	Full
Beef			1	1	2	3	3
Lamb			1	1	2	2	3
Veal, Pork	1	2	3	2	2	1	
Goose, Duck, Game			1	2	2	3	3
Chicken, Turkey	2	2	3	1	1	1	
Fish	2	3	2		1		
Shellfish	3	2	2	1			

How To Pronounce Texas Premium Wines

Cabernet Sauvignon	kab-er-**nay so**-vee-nyon
Chardonnay	**shar**-done-nay
Chenin Blanc	**shen**-an **blon**
Claret	clare-**ette**
Gamay Beaujolais	**gam**-may **bo**-zho-lay
Gewurztraminer	geh-**vertz**-tra-**mee**-ner
Johannisberg Riesling	yo-**hohn**-iss-berg **rees**-ling
Merlot	mare-**low**
Pinot Noir	**pee**-no **nowahr**
Sauvignon Blanc	**so**-vee-nyon blon
Zinfandel	**zin**-fun-dell

Texas wines are growing in popularity for several reasons. First, the hot climate grape varietals are a perfect match for the spicy cuisine that Texans love! Second, many of Texas' vineyards are now more than ten years old, and the fruit is in its prime. Third, Texas wine makers are maturing at their craft and are making wines that match the Texas palate.

For additional information about the Texas Wine and Grape Growers Association and the "Friends of Texas Wine," contact the executive office at 701 South Main Street, Grapevine, Texas, 76051, call 817-424-0570, or visit their web site at www.twgga.org.